The Vietnamese Cookbook

BY DIANA MY TRAN PHOTOGRAPHS BY STEVE RAYMER

The Vietnamese
Cookbook

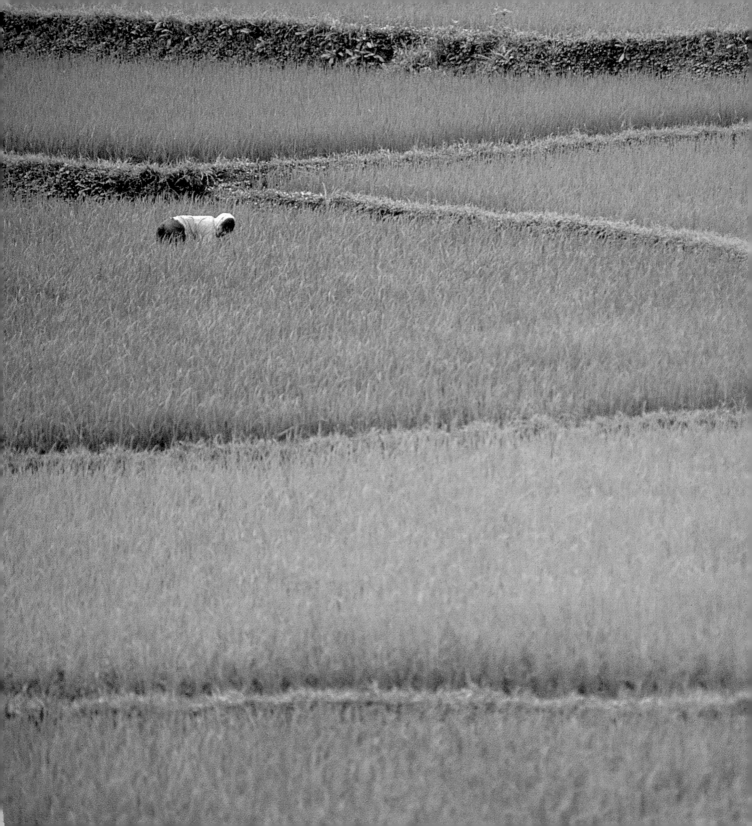

Acknowledgments

My first year in America, I so often wondered what my future would hold. My family struggled, but we always appreciated this wonderful land. As I write this book, I cannot help but be thrilled at how much we have accomplished since those first days. I owe a great gratitude to America, the land of opportunities.

I dedicate this book to all my American friends in Carlisle, Pennsylvania, especially Sally and Carl DeAngelo, Mary and Tracy Sanders, Ilene and Charles, Chris, Bill Williams and many more. I feel very fortunate to have so many friends who welcomed my family and me with wide-open arms, showing us the most wonderful friendship mankind has to offer.

I would like to express my deepest gratitude to my publisher, Kathleen Hughes, of Capital Books, Inc. and Ruina Judd, my agent and producer, of Judd Publishing, Inc. without whom I never could have completed my dream. Also to Penne Korth, who introduced me to this opportunity and to Ann Yonkers for her great advice and support.

Special appreciation to Steve Raymer my talented photographer, and the book's designer, Donna Sicklesmith-Anderson.

I am also very grateful to my staff at Diana's Couture & Bridal of Georgetown. They have worked hours of overtime while I was working on this project. Thanks to Mr. and Mrs. Nguyen Ngoc Bich, Ms. Kim Oanh, Long Vu, Ann Yick— all my friends and clients at Diana's for all their support and encouragement.

Many thanks go to all my teachers and classmates in St. Paul Institution Francais in Vietnam.

Especially, I thank my family, my parents and my two aunts—"Ma Ba" and "Ma Nam"—I owe them my whole life's gratitude. I thank my son, John Tran, for all his technical computer help and for being such a great taster. I thank my daughter, Diana Tran, who did a great job with all the cooking and cleanup assistance. Last but not least, I thank my husband, Triet Tran, for all his support and patience. I love them all very much.

—DIANA MY TRAN

The Vietnamese
Cookbook

Introduction

DIANA MY TRAN

Born in Vietnam, I lived with an aunt and uncle in Saigon so that I could attend the best French-speaking schools. I had a very finicky appetite and was always indulged by my family. My aunt would cook anything I demanded to satisfy my whims. On weekends, my parents would come to visit. We often went out to eat at restaurants as a treat, sampling French, Chinese and Indian cuisine.

I come from a large family. We had numerous parties, celebrations and family gatherings. The night before an event, members of the family gathered at my parents' home. My aunts and uncles brought live chickens from their farms and freshly picked produce from their gardens. My sister was a *tour de force*. She prepared the menu and the grocery list and did much of the cooking. The noise from the kitchen would wake me in the early morning and I would join my mother, sisters and aunts, sometimes helping them prepare the food, but more often just tasting my sister's cooking as it came hot from the wok. When I look back on these family get togethers, I know I will never forget the aroma, the fresh foods, the laughter and the happy times.

In September 1975, my family and I arrived in Carlisle, Pennsylvania on a bright, sunny, autumn day. The clear sky, the light breeze, the trees with leaves just beginning to turn to gold, seemed to welcome us to America. My first child, a son, was born just a few weeks after our arrival.

The first few months were difficult. Though still very homesick, I tried hard to take care of our family of five which included my parents-in-law, my husband and our baby. Everything bewildered me. Thank heavens for all our wonderful friends in Carlisle who gave my family the warmest of welcomes as well as unstinting help. We were one of the first Vietnamese refugee families to arrive in their town. Vietnamese culture was interesting to them, and I loved sharing tales of Vietnam.

Inevitably, Vietnamese cooking was a hot topic. Deeply touched by their hospitality, I loved to invite our new friends over to try traditional Vietnamese dishes. Everyone loved spring rolls and the dipping sauce—*Nuoc Mam*, Vietnam's famous fish sauce. Occasionally they would sip the sauce like soup, spooning it straight from the bowl—too good to leave a drop!

Cooking Vietnamese dishes at that time was a challenge because there were no Asian food stores in the area. Most of the time, I could not find the traditional ingredients and had to make substitutions, but the food turned out just fine. The American supermarket amazed me—the size of the store and the variety of goods. In Vietnam, we shopped at an open-air market where the only produce was home grown and freshly cut.

A year later, we moved to the Virginia suburbs of Washington DC. We settled into a small apartment. My husband became a full-time college student. Washington had a much larger Vietnamese community than Carlisle so there were numerous Vietnamese and Asian markets.

The first time I visited a Vietnamese grocery store in Virginia, tears came to my eyes. It was such a joy to see the familiar ingredients again.

The availability of Vietnamese ingredients started me on a whole new career—cooking, baking and sewing at home. With the baby, I kept very busy and it certainly helped with the family income. I also trained as a bilingual secretary and soon landed my first "real" job which kept me even busier.

In June 1982, my second child, a daughter, was born, and my life changed again. I opened my own design and dressmaking business in Georgetown. After struggling in the early years, I have built up a wide clientele. My customers come from all walks of life, but they all appreciate stylish, well-fitting clothes and adhere to a healthy diet. While fitting them I share my secret for staying in shape—Vietnamese food—lighter and lower in fat than Western food, with a much higher proportion of vegetables. By far their favorite recipes are Chicken Salad, *Goi Ga,* and Clear Vegetable

Soup, *Canh Rau*—delicious, low in fat, fast and easy to prepare.

Today, more than 20 years after leaving Vietnam, I am a professional business woman, and my time for cooking is as limited as it ever was when I was scraping by as a new immigrant. Traditional Vietnamese food can take time and effort to prepare—time I usually don't have. I want to keep our family heritage alive, especially for my children, so I have created my own easier versions of Vietnamese dishes, tailored to the American busy lifestyle. Keeping the original tastes and textures, my recipes make use of ingredients easily found in local supermarkets. It is a great pleasure for me to share these with you, and I hope you will find cooking Vietnamese specialties to be as easy as cooking Western food. This book will show you step-by-step how to create healthy delights of Vietnamese cuisine—fast!

GETTING STARTED

Equipment

Vietnamese cooking requires a few special utensils, which are readily available. You will need a wok, stir-fry pans, a steamer, a food processor, two soup pots, saucepans and, if possible, an electric rice-cooker. Rice is the most important of Vietnam's foods, I highly recommend buying an electric rice cooker. It will make cooking rice virtually foolproof and save you a great deal of time. Sharp knives and/or a cleaver for cutting and chopping are essential.

Ingredients

Vietnamese cuisine is becoming very popular in America. Many of the essential ingredients such as fish sauce, oyster sauce, soy sauce, hoisin sauce, all types of rice, Asian spices including five-spice powder, curry powder and peppers, traditional Asian herbs, rice papers and wonton wrappers, a variety of noodles including bean thread vermicelli and many rice noodles, dried Asian mushrooms, can be found in local supermarkets, as well as in Asian markets.

CLOCKWISE FROM TOP: bottled red pepper sauce (also in small dish); garlic cloves; yucca; cilantro; fresh ginger; lemongrass; star anise; sesame seeds (in wooden scoop); dried red peppers (chiles); mint; bean thread noodles; black peppercorns, ground red pepper, ground ginger and five-spice powder (clockwise from upper left, all four in dish); basil (with dark stem); dried mushrooms; cayang; rau om (tucked under dish); culantro or ngo gai (on noodles); rice vermicelli noodles; fresh red pepper (chile); and CENTER: dried mung beans (in square dish).

Diana's Vietnamese Cooking Starter Kit of spices and sauces may be ordered via e-mail at **vietchef@hotmail.com** or by calling **202-333-5689**.

Rice

In Vietnam, rice is considered a gift from God. When I was a little girl my mother would not allow me to leave the table until I had finished every grain of rice in my bowl. She said by eating all the rice I was showing gratitude to God for giving us such a valuable gift. This tradition is passed down from generation to generation and I have passed it along to my children here in America.

Rice is absolutely essential at every Asian meal, more so than bread in the Western diet. A traditional Vietnamese meal consists mainly of rice accompanied by a salty dish of seafood or meat, vegetables and/or a composed salad. Cooking rice is an art, but one that isn't too hard to master. An electric rice cooker makes perfect rice—which should be moist and fluffy—a snap.

Jasmine rice, the traditional, common everyday rice, is preferred by most Vietnamese for its aroma, but any long-grained rice will suffice if it is cooked with the correct amount of water.

Glutinous rice, also called sticky rice, has a silky, sticky texture. Glutinous rice can be long-, short- or round-grained with a creamy, sticky consistency when cooked.

Black rice is a dark, long-grained rice. It takes longer to cook and has a slightly crunchy texture and a wonderful nutty taste. Often compared to American wild rice, black rice is a dramatic accompaniment for roasted meats, poultry, game and other Western dishes.

PLAIN RICE [Cơm Trắng]

Serves 4 to 6

My father always said he would rather have perfectly cooked rice and a plain bowl of fish sauce than badly cooked rice with any number of delicious entrées. This also holds true for my husband and me. Plain rice is key in traditional Vietnamese families.

2 cups long-grained Jasmine rice

2¼ cups water

1 Wash the rice until the water runs clear, then drain.

2 In a small nonstick saucepan, add rice and water. Bring to a boil, turn down heat to medium and cook until all water is absorbed—about seven minutes, stirring gently once or twice. Cover tightly, turn heat to *very low* and cook until tender, about 15 to 20 minutes.

3 Before serving, fluff rice with chopsticks or a fork.

TO SERVE: Vietnamese serve rice with any entrée in individual small bowls, with chopsticks.

NOTES:

CLOCKWISE FROM TOP:
Black Rice, Lemon Rice,
Mung Bean Sticky Rice
and Tomato Rice.

TOMATO RICE [Cơm Sốt Cà]

Serves 4 to 6

Vietnam was a French colony for 100 years, so it's not surprising that our traditional food was deeply influenced by French cooking. This variation of Plain Rice has French roots in its use of garlic, butter and tomato sauce.

1 Wash the rice until the water runs clear, then drain.

2 Mix water, salt, garlic, melted butter, tomato sauce and rice in a nonstick saucepan and bring to a boil. Turn heat down to *very low,* stir gently, cover tightly and cook until tender, about 15 to 20 minutes.

3 Before serving, stir with chopsticks or a fork to assure an even moisture.

TO SERVE: Serve steaming hot with any seafood, meat and chicken dishes.

2 cups long-grained Jasmine rice

2 cups water

¼ teaspoon salt

1 teaspoon garlic powder

1 tablespoon butter, *melted or* oil

2 tablespoons tomato sauce

LEMON RICE [Cơm Chanh]

Serves 4 to 6

I combined two things I love—rice and lemon—for this dish. It has a marvelous fresh fragrance.

1 Wash the rice until the water runs clear, then drain.

2 Mix water, salt, melted butter and rice in a nonstick saucepan and bring to a boil. Turn heat down to *very low,* stir gently, cover tightly and cook until tender, about 15 to 20 minutes.

3 Add lemon zest and juice and mix lightly with chopsticks or a fork.

TO SERVE: Serve steaming hot with seafood and chicken dishes.

2 cups long-grained Jasmine rice

2 cups water

½ teaspoon salt

1 tablespoon butter, *melted or* oil

zest of half a lemon

1 teaspoon lemon juice

SHRIMP FRIED RICE [Cơm Chiên Tôm]

Serves 4 to 6

I hate leftovers. Every day I want to eat something fresh. But this is a great way to use extra leftover plain rice. And, in fact, this dish is better using the refrigerated rice, which is drier than just-cooked rice.

1 Heat 1½ teaspoons of oil in a sauté pan, pour in egg and make one thin omelet.

2 Heat one tablespoon of oil in the same pan and cook garlic with half the chopped onion until light brown. Add shrimp and stir-fry about five minutes. Transfer mixture to a large bowl.

3 Heat the rest of the oil in the sauté pan and sauté the remaining chopped onion with the scallions. Add cooked rice and heat through, stirring constantly. Add shrimp, oyster sauce or soy sauce, salt and pepper and stir-fry until rice turns a golden brown.

TO SERVE: Garnish with sprigs of cilantro.

2½ tablespoons oil

1 egg, *beaten*

2 garlic cloves, *minced*

1 small head onion, *coarsely chopped*

10 medium shrimp, *coarsely chopped*

2 scallions, *coarsely chopped*

4 cups cooked rice

1 tablespoon oyster sauce or 1 teaspoon soy sauce

¼ teaspoon salt

½ teaspoon black pepper

cilantro sprigs for garnish

BLACK RICE [Xôi Nếp Than]
Serves 3 to 4

In Vietnam, black rice is served mostly plain for breakfast on the go or mixed with shredded coconut and sesame seeds or crushed peanuts, salt and sugar as an afternoon snack. Americans will find this Black Rice an excellent alternative to wild rice…with its similar exotic nutty taste.

1 Soak black rice in water for at least four hours or, preferably, overnight, then drain.

2 Combine black rice and water in a nonstick saucepan.,Bring to a boil. Turn heat to medium and simmer until all water is absorbed, about 40 minutes. If you prefer, use a rice steamer. Place rice in steamer over boiling water and steam 40 mintues until tender.

3 Before serving, fluff rice with chopsticks or a fork. Garnish with shredded coconut and sesame seeds or crushed peanuts.

TO SERVE: Enjoy Black Rice with Vietnamese or American dishes—especially baked meats, poultry or game.

1 cup black rice

2 cups water

GARNISH: *(optional)*

1 cup shredded coconut

1 tablespoon sesame seeds *or* crushed peanuts

STICKY RICE [Xôi Nếp]

Serves 4 to 6

Unlike plain rice, Vietnamese prepare sticky rice dishes only as gourmet rice dishes on special occasions, mostly for family gatherings. However, street vendors often have a variety of sticky rice offerings served with shredded coconut, salt and sesame seeds...usually in the early morning. Sticky Rice has become popular for breakfast on the go or as a morning or evening snack.

2 cups glutinous rice

2 cups water

1 teaspoon oil

½ teaspoon salt

1 Wash the rice until the water runs clear, then drain.

2 In a small nonstick saucepan, add rice, water, oil and salt. Bring to a boil, turn down heat to medium and cook until all water is absorbed— about seven minutes, stirring gently once or twice. Cover tightly, turn heat to *very low* and cook until tender, about 15 to 20 minutes.

3 Before serving, fluff rice with chopsticks or a fork.

TO SERVE: Sticky Rice may be served with any barbequed meat dishes, and is used as the base for many dessert dishes.

NOTES:

MUNG BEAN STICKY RICE [Xôi Vò]

Serves 4 to 6

My father-in-law came from North Vietnam. He was very traditional, except that he loved to cook. His specialty, which he produced impeccably, was Mung Bean Sticky Rice. Each and every grain of rice was perfectly coated with mung bean. Though the grains look dry and separate, they taste soft and fluffy. My father-in-law passed away four years ago. I include this recipe in his memory.

1 cup mung beans

2 cups round-grained glutinous rice

⅔ cup water

½ teaspoon salt

1 tablespoon oil

1 Soak mung beans and glutinous rice in two separate pans for at least three hours in warm water, or preferably overnight.

2 Rinse in a colander and thoroughly drain mung beans. Combine water and mung beans in a nonstick saucepan. Do not cover the saucepan. Bring to a boil, turn heat to medium-low and stir gently, until all water is absorbed—about seven minutes. Cover the saucepan tightly. Turn heat to *very low* and cook until dry and fluffy, about 10 additional minutes. Set aside to cool.

3 Using the back of a large spoon, mash mung beans to a paste.

4 Drain rice thoroughly until dry, then toss rice with mung bean paste, salt and oil, until well combined. Place mixture in a steamer and steam 20 minutes over boiling water. Spread rice on a cookie sheet and using chopsticks or a fork, fluff rice to separate the grains.

TO SERVE: Serve by itself or to accompany meat dishes. To serve as a sweet snack or dessert, sprinkle with shredded coconut, toasted sesame seeds, and a little sugar.

NOTES:

PEANUT STICKY RICE [Xôi Đậu Phộng]

Serves 4 to 6

In Vietnam, breakfast might be a bowl of soup, a bowl of fried rice, a sandwich on French bread, or just a banana leaf cone of sticky rice for an inexpensive breakfast on the run.

1 Soak raw peanuts and glutinous rice in two separate pans for at least three hours in warm water, or preferably overnight, then drain.

2 In a saucepan, cover peanuts with water and bring to a boil. Simmer for 20 minutes.

3 Using a nonstick saucepan, combine cooked peanuts, rice, water, coconut milk, salt and oil and bring to a boil. Immediately turn down the heat and stir gently. Cover tightly, turn the heat to *very low* and cook until all water is absorbed—about 20 minutes. Before serving, fluff rice with chopsticks or a fork. If using a steamer, omit water. Combine cooked peanuts, rice, peanuts, coconut milk, salt and oil. Steam 20 minutes over boiling water.

TO SERVE: Garnish with shredded coconut. If you wish, add crushed peanuts, sesame seeds, a little salt and/or sugar to taste. This dish can be served by itself or with an entrée.

NOTES:

1 cup raw peanuts

2 cups glutinous rice

1 cup water

½ cup coconut milk

½ teaspoon salt

1 tablespoon oil

GARNISH:

½ cup shredded coconut

2 tablespoons crushed roasted peanuts *(optional)*

2 tablespoons sesame seeds *(optional)*

Sauces

A variety of sauces accompany every meal in
Vietnam. The most important Vietnamese sauce
is Fish Sauce, Nuoc Mam. Fish sauce is served
with everything. It is always on the table, just as salt
and pepper are in America.

My aunt owned a wholesale seafood business. She also
produced fish sauce. The process begins with layers of fish being
placed in a large crock or vat-like container. Salt is placed with the
fish in layers separated by netting. The salt preserves the fish as it ferments, dissolves and liquefies.
The liquid passes through each layer of netting, being filtered as it makes its way slowly to the
bottom of the container. The liquid then goes, drop by drop, out a small hole—very dark and salty.

This concentrate is boiled and refiltered yielding a clear liquid. It is quite intense, like
concentrated perfume, and is usually mixed with lime or lemon juice or a little vinegar, water and
sugar. Every family has a different version, just as in America everyone has a slightly different recipe
for salad dressing. If you can't find fish sauce, substitute soy sauce for making my sauces.

Soy sauce is a dark brown, briny sauce of naturally fermented soybeans, aged for up to two
years. Vegetarians use soy sauce instead of fish sauce.

Hoisin sauce is also made from soybeans and numerous spices. It is dark reddish-brown,
slightly sweet, with a thick, jam-like consistency. Hoisin sauce, with my variations, is traditionally
served with Garden Rolls, Vegetable Rolls, Grilled Sesame Beef and with Pho.

SWEET AND SOUR FISH SAUCE [Nước Mắm]

Yield: 1 cup

Sweet and Sour Fish Sauce accompanies almost every savory dish in Vietnamese cuisine. It is as ubiquitous as salt in Western cuisine.

1 In a small bowl, mix garlic, sugar, citrus juice, water and fish sauce until the sugar is completely dissolved. Stir in ground red chile pepper, if you like a little "hot."

Serve with almost every entrée.

NOTES:

2 garlic cloves,
   finely minced

3 tablespoons sugar

2 tablespoons lime
   or lemon juice

½ cup warm water

6 tablespoons fish sauce

½ teaspoon ground red
   chile pepper *(optional)*

SWEET AND SOUR GINGER FISH SAUCE [Nước Mắm Gừng]

Yield: 1 cup

1 Mix all ingredients together thoroughly. Include the ground red pepper if you like the heat.

Serve with fish and poultry dishes.

NOTES:

1 garlic clove,
   finely minced

3 tablespoons sugar

2 tablespoons lime
   or lemon juice

¼ cup warm water

7 tablespoons fish sauce

1 tablespoon fresh ginger,
   finely minced

½ teaspoon ground red
   chile pepper *(optional)*

CLOCKWISE FROM UPPER LEFT: Sweet and Sour Fish Sauce, Sweet and Sour Soy Sauce, Pineapple Tomato Sauce and Peanut Hoisin Sauce.

SWEET AND SOUR SOY SAUCE [Nước Tương Chua Ngọt]

Yield: 1 cup

Sweet and Sour Soy Sauce is a substitute for Sweet and Sour Fish Sauce for Buddhist vegetarians who have dietary restrictions that go beyond the avoidance of meat, fish and products made from meat and fish, such as fish sauce. Their beliefs prohibit five herbs or vegetables—garlic, onion, scallion, leek and chives. Regular Buddhists believe that vegetarian food has a cleansing and calming effect on the body, and many choose to eat vegetarian food for two, four, or 10 days of the lunar calendar. This is not considered a fast. Each person is at liberty to eat as much or as little as he or she chooses. Dishes often include tofu and rice.

2 garlic cloves, *finely minced*

2 tablespoons sugar

2 tablespoons lime *or lemon juice*

½ cup warm water

7 tablespoons soy sauce

½ teaspoon ground red chile pepper *(optional)*

1 In a small bowl, mix garlic, sugar, citrus juice, water and soy sauce until the sugar is completely dissolved. Stir in ground red chile pepper, if you like a little "hot." Buddhist vegetarians may omit garlic.

Serve with any entrée calling for Sweet and Sour Fish Sauce.

HONEY SAUCE [Sốt Mật]

Yield: 1 cup

1 Combine honey, sugar, fish sauce, water and cornstarch in a small saucepan. Cook over low heat. Stir constantly until the mixture becomes thick. For a spicier sauce, add ground red pepper or red chile paste. Garnish with cilantro leaves before serving.

Serve with Shrimp Tails (page 34) and Shrimp Toast Rolls (page 35).

NOTES:

6 tablespoons honey

3 tablespoons sugar

6 tablespoons fish sauce

½ tablespoon water

1 teaspoon cornstarch

1 teaspoon ground red pepper *or* red chile paste *(optional)*

cilantro leaves for garnish

PEANUT HOISIN SAUCE [Tương Đậu Phộng]

Yield: 2½ cups

1 In a saucepan, mix the stock, milk, hoisin sauce, red chile sauce, peanut butter and sugar. Bring it to a boil and immediately turn the heat down to low.

2 In a small bowl, mix water and cornstarch. Pour into the saucepan and stir constantly until the sauce is thick and creamy. Garnish with crushed peanuts before serving.

Serve with Garden Rolls (page 30) and Vegetable Rolls (page 33).

NOTES:

1½ cup shrimp and pork stock

½ cup milk

3 tablespoons hoisin sauce

1 tablespoon red chile sauce *(optional)*

2 tablespoons crunchy peanut butter

1 tablespoon sugar

½ cup water

1½ tablespoons cornstarch

⅓ cup crushed peanuts for garnish

SPICY HOISIN SAUCE [Tương Đen]

Yield: ½ cup

1 Mix hoisin sauce and water until smooth. Stir in ground red pepper or red chile paste to taste.

Serve with Vegetable Rolls (page 33), Chicken *or* Beef Noodle Soup (pages 53, 54), and Lemongrass Ground Beef on Skewers (page 85).

4 tablespoons hoisin sauce

¼ cup water

2 teaspoons ground red pepper *or* red chile paste

PINEAPPLE TOMATO SAUCE [Sốt Thơm Cà Chua]

Yield: 2 cups

1 Use food processor or blender to puree tomato.

2 In a small bowl, mix pineapple juice and cornstarch.

3 Heat oil in a small saucepan and stir-fry garlic, onion and scallions until fragrant. Stir in tomato puree, pineapple-cornstarch mixture, sugar and fish sauce. Simmer over medium-low heat. Sauce is ready when it becomes clear and thick.

Serve with Shrimp Tails (page 34), Meatballs (page 74), Stuffed Tomatoes (page 75) and Stuffed Tofu with Shrimp and Pork Paste (page 79).

1 medium tomato

¾ cup pineapple juice

2 teaspoons cornstarch

1 teaspoon oil

1 garlic clove, *finely minced*

½ medium onion, *finely chopped*

2 scallions, *finely sliced*

1 tablespoon sugar

3 tablespoons fish sauce

VINEGAR SALAD DRESSING [Sốt Dầu Dấm]

Yield: 1 cup

1 In a medium bowl, beat together the white vinegar, olive oil, water, salt, pepper and sugar. When sugar is completely dissolved, pour over the garlic and thinly sliced onion and toss well.

Serve this dressing with all salads, whether Western or Vietnamese.

½ cup white vinegar

1 teaspoon olive oil

¼ cup water

½ teaspoon salt

½ teaspoon black pepper

1½ tablespoons sugar

2 garlic cloves, *finely minced*

1 small onion, red *or* white, *thinly sliced*

Appetizers & Salads

SPRING ROLLS [Chả Giò]

Serves 6 to 8 (15 rolls)

Spring rolls are the most famous appetizer in Vietnam, especially as a finger food for parties. The recipe that follows is my simplified version, as the original recipe takes a great deal of time to prepare.

1 If dried mushrooms are used, soak them in hot water for one hour, trim hard stems and pat dry.

2 Using a food processor, coarsely chop mushrooms, scallions, garlic and onion. Transfer to a large mixing bowl and, using a fork, lightly stir in the crabmeat, ground pork, salt, pepper, sugar and cornstarch. Beat one egg and stir into the mixture, or knead gently by hand. Let mixture rest for 15 minutes in the refrigerator.

3 On your work surface, assemble the filling, the rice papers, a dampened dish towel or several dampened paper towels, a pastry brush and a small bowl of warm water. Working with three rice wrappers at a time, dampen entire surface of each rice paper with a pastry brush dipped in warm water. Place rice papers on a cookie sheet, let soften for one minute, then cover with the damp towel.

4 Place 1½ tablespoons filling on each rice paper, about one inch from the edge nearest you, then form into rolls three inches long. Fold in rice paper on each side, then fold over the remaining edge to completely enclose filling. Roll up and press the far edge firmly in place. Continue with remaining ingredients.

5 If using egg roll skins, coat edge of egg roll skin with beaten egg. Then continue as above for rice papers.

6 Heat oil over medium heat until hot. Gently add rolls and fry, turning them frequently, until they are an even golden brown. Remove to paper towels to drain. Transfer to a heated platter and serve warm, accompanied by Sweet and Sour Fish Sauce (page 24) and Garden Salad (page 63).

FILLING:

4 dried Chinese black mushrooms *or* 6 fresh white mushrooms

3 scallions

2 garlic cloves

½ cup onion

½ cup fresh backfin *or* lump crabmeat

1 cup ground pork *or* chicken

½ teaspoon salt

½ teaspoon black pepper, *freshly ground*

½ teaspoon sugar

½ teaspoon cornstarch

2 eggs

15 6-inch rice papers (Banh Trang) *or* 15 8" x 8" egg roll skins

2 cups oil

Sweet and Sour Fish Sauce (page 24)

Garden Salad (page 63)

GARDEN ROLLS [Gỏi Cuốn]

Serves 6 to 8 (15 rolls)

In Saigon, when the weather gets really hot and sticky, garden rolls are the perfect cool dish for an afternoon snack.

1 Bring a large saucepan of water to a boil. Add rice vermicelli, and stirring gently, cook until the noodles are transparent and soft—about five minutes. Drain and rinse under cold running water. Drain again thoroughly and set aside.

2 Cut the pork into one-inch-thick slices. In a medium saucepan, simmer pork strips in the 1½ cups water for about 20 minutes, until well done. Remove pork strips and reserve stock. When cool, cut slices into narrow strips. Using the same saucepan, heat reserved stock, add shrimp and cook about five minutes, until pink and curled. Remove shrimp, cool, devein and set aside. Reserve stock for use in Peanut Hoisin Sauce (page 26).

3 Wash lettuce leaves and tear them in half. Wash garlic chives and cut in two long strips. Wash bean sprouts and drain thoroughly. Strip leaves from mint, basil and cilantro sprigs; wash and pat dry.

4 On your work surface, assemble all ingredients, as well as a pastry brush, a bowl of warm water and a dampened dish towel or paper towel. Use the pastry brush dipped into warm water to dampen the entire surface of three pieces of rice paper, putting each on the damp towel. Working with three rice papers at a time, place the following in a six-inch row one inch from the edge nearest you: half a Romaine lettuce leaf, a few herbs, a little vermicelli and three pieces of meat and shrimp. Fold the left and right sides of the rice paper inward. Insert two garlic chive strips about seven inches long. Fold the bottom, nearest edge over the filling, while pressing down the mixture, and roll as tightly as possible to the top edge. Repeat the same procedure with the remaining ingredients. Cover rolls with plastic wrap so they don't dry out and set aside until serving time.

4 ounces dry rice vermicelli *(to yield about 1 cup cooked)*

½ pound lean, boneless pork

1½ cups water

30 medium size shrimp

10 leaves lettuce *(such as Romaine)*

10 sprigs garlic chives

2 cups bean sprouts

5 mint sprigs

5 basil sprigs

5 cilantro sprigs

15 8-inch round rice papers

red chile sauce

Peanut Hoisin Sauce (page 26) *or* Spicy Hoisin Sauce (page 27)

TO SERVE: Sprinkle Garden Rolls with crushed peanuts and pass red chile sauce separately. Each person should be served an individual bowl of Peanut Hoisin Sauce (page 26).

BEEF ROLLS [Bì Bò Cuốn]

Serves 6 to 8 (15 rolls)

When you wish to have a light meal that is a little heavier than salad, this appetizer will fill the bill.

1 Over medium flame, heat oil in a frying pan. Brown garlic, then stir in chopped onion and cook until soft. Add ground beef, crushed peanuts, salt, pepper and sugar and stir until meat is well done.

2 Proceed as for Garden Rolls (page 30), beginning at instruction number **3**.

TO SERVE: Serve with Sweet and Sour Fish Sauce (page 24).

NOTES:

1 tablespoon oil

2 garlic cloves

1 medium onion, *chopped*

1 cup ground beef

¼ cup peanuts, *crushed*

¼ teaspoon salt

¼ teaspoon black pepper

¼ teaspoon sugar

10 leaves Romaine lettuce

5 mint sprigs

5 basil sprigs

5 cilantro sprigs

2 cups bean sprouts

1 cup cooked rice vermicelli

15 8-inch round rice papers

Sweet and Sour Fish Sauce (page 24)

VEGETABLE ROLLS [Bó Bía Chay]

Serves 6 to 8 (15 rolls)

This is a vegetarian version of the Garden Rolls.

1 Heat oil in a frying pan and stir-fry carrots, cabbage, mushrooms, onion and peanuts until soft. Add tofu, salt, pepper and sugar. Toss gently and taste for seasoning.

2 Proceed as for Garden Rolls (page 30), beginning at instruction number **3**.

TO SERVE: Serve with Peanut Hoisin Sauce (page 26) or Spicy Hoisin Sauce (page 27).

NOTES:

1 tablespoon oil

1 cup shredded carrots

1 cup shredded cabbage

½ cup chopped white mushrooms

1 medium onion, *chopped*

¼ cup peanuts, *crushed*

2 4" x 6" hard tofu, *raw or fried, sliced into thin strips*

¼ teaspoon salt

¼ teaspoon black pepper

¼ teaspoon sugar

10 leaves lettuce (*such as Romaine*)

10 sprigs garlic chives

2 cups bean sprouts

5 mint sprigs

5 basil sprigs

5 cilantro sprigs

1 cup cooked rice vermicelli

15 8-inch round rice papers

Peanut Hoisin Sauce (page 26) *or* Spicy Hoisin Sauce (page 27)

SHRIMP TAILS [Hoành Thánh Cuốn Tôm]

Serves 6 to 10 (20 rolls)

When we arrived in America, rice papers were not very easy to find.
A good substitute was wonton wrappers, which are used in this recipe.

1 Thaw 20 egg roll skins or wonton wrappers. Remaining egg roll skin/ wonton wrappers may be frozen for future use.

2 Put the 10 medium shrimp, onion, scallions, salt, pepper, sugar and cornstarch in a food processor and grind at medium speed to form a paste. Remove the paste to a mixing bowl and stir in the ground pork. Gently knead filling with your fingers or a wooden spoon. Refrigerate for 10 minutes.

3 Place wrappers on a cutting board or a plate. Moisten edges of wrapper with beaten egg. Use one teaspoon of filling and spread it in a two-inch line diagonally across the wonton wrapper. Put one whole shrimp on top and gently fold up and press together the three corners, starting first with the top and then the two sides. Roll. Repeat with remaining ingredients.

4 Heat oil, in a deep saucepan over medium heat. Carefully add rolls one at a time and deep-fry until light golden brown. Drain on paper towel to remove excess oil and keep warm.

TO SERVE: Serve with Honey Sauce (page 26) or Pineapple Tomato Sauce (page 27).

20 6" x 6" egg roll skins
or wonton wrappers

10 medium shrimp,
shelled (leaving tail intact), and deveined

20 medium shrimp,
shelled and deveined

1 small onion, red *or* white, *finely chopped*

1 scallion, *finely chopped*

½ teaspoon salt

½ teaspoon black pepper

½ teaspoon sugar

½ teaspoon cornstarch

¾ cup ground pork

1 egg, *beaten*

2 cups olive oil

Honey Sauce (page 26)
or Pineapple Tomato Sauce (page 27)

SHRIMP TOAST ROLLS [Bánh Mì Cuốn Tôm]

Serves 8 to 10

I love to try out new cooking ideas. This particular appetizer is a new version of the traditional recipe for shrimp toast. By rolling the bread out flat, the toast rolls will absorb much less oil—thereby reducing the fat content. This recipe makes a terrific finger food for parties.

1 Lightly beat eggs with the salt. Divide beaten egg by four, and using a small preheated frying pan, heat oil and make four thin egg sheets.

2 Purée the shrimp, garlic, onion, salt, pepper and cornstarch in a food processor to form a thick paste. Transfer to a large bowl and refrigerate for 10 minutes.

3 Using a rolling pin, roll out and flatten each slice of bread.

4 Spread shrimp paste thinly on bread, covering the entire surface. Cut each egg sheet into four-inch strips. Place strips on shrimp paste and roll tightly. Repeat with remaining ingredients.

5 In a deep fryer, over medium heat, heat oil until hot. Gently lower bread rolls into the hot oil and deep fry until golden brown. Remove to paper towels to drain.

TO SERVE: Slice rolls into bite-sized pieces and place on a serving platter. Garnish with lettuce leaves and a tomato rose. These rolls can be served alone or accompanied by Sweet and Sour Fish Sauce (page 24) and Honey Sauce (page 26).

NOTES:

2 eggs

pinch of salt

1 tablespoon oil

30 shrimp, *shelled and deveined*

2 garlic cloves, *minced*

¼ cup onion, *minced*

½ teaspoon salt

½ teaspoon black pepper

½ teaspoon cornstarch

10 slices white bread, *crusts trimmed*

2 cups olive oil

GARNISH:

lettuce leaves

tomato peel rose

Sweet and Sour Fish Sauce (page 24)

Honey Sauce (page 26)

SHRIMP MUNG BEAN RICE CAKES [Bánh Ích Tôm Thịt]

Serves 6 to 8 (24 cakes)

This appetizer is always a success at parties. My son, John Tran, said the only rice cakes he loves are the ones his mother makes. For me, this is reason enough to call them my specialty.

1 Soak dry mung beans in a saucepan of warm water. Set aside for one hour.

2 Rinse mung beans thoroughly in a colander and drain.

3 In a nonstick saucepan, mix mung beans and the 1 cup water. Bring to the boil, uncovered, over medium-low heat, stirring gently. Cover saucepan tightly, turn heat to very low and cook until mung beans are dry and fluffy, approximately 20 minutes. Cool and set aside.

4 In a large frying pan, heat oil and brown garlic and onion. Add pork, shrimp, salt, pepper and sugar, and stir-fry for five minutes. Add cooked mung beans and fish sauce. Stirring constantly, mash beans with the back of a large spoon until all ingredients are well mixed. Cool and set aside for 10 minutes. Meanwhile, prepare dough.

5 In a large bowl, mix glutinous rice flour with the water. Then knead until smooth. Divide dough into 24 even portions.

6 Prepare your work station. Lightly oil the 24 aluminum foil squares. Pour remaining oil into a small bowl.

7 Oil your hands and form the mung bean mixture into 24 balls, 1½-inch diameter.

8 Use your palms to flatten each ball of rice-flour dough into a two-inch circle. Place a mung bean ball into the center of the circle of dough, molding dough around it to enclose the bean ball completely. With oiled palms, gently roll each ball clockwise until it is smooth and rounded.

FILLING:

1 cup dry mung beans

1 cup water

1 tablespoon oil

2 garlic cloves, *minced*

1 cup onion, *finely chopped*

1 cup pork shoulder, *cooked and thinly sliced*

10 medium shrimp, *shelled and chopped*

½ teaspoon salt

½ teaspoon black pepper

½ teaspoon sugar

1 teaspoon fish sauce

RICE CAKE DOUGH:

4 cups (1 pound) glutinous rice flour

2 cups warm water

2 tablespoons oil

aluminum foil, *cut into 24 2" x 2" squares*

Scallion Sauté (page 91) for garnish

Sweet and Sour Fish Sauce (page 24)

Place each ball on an oiled foil square. The oiled squares keep the cakes from sticking to the steamer.

9 Arrange eight mung bean balls one inch apart in a steamer. Bring water to a boil, cover and steam each batch for 10 minutes, and set aside until cool enough to handle.

TO SERVE: Oil your hands first because the balls are very sticky, then remove foil and arrange the balls on a lightly oiled plate. The mung bean balls can be served alone, garnished with Scallion Sauté (page 91) and/or with Sweet and Sour Fish Sauce (page 24.)

BAKED HOISIN SAUCE CHICKEN WINGS [Cánh Gà Nướng Tương]

Serves 5 to 7

When I was a secretary, I had a Chinese boss (and best friend) who introduced this wonderful appetizer to me. It was always a great hit at the office lunches. She always reminded me to "stop and eat" when life was hectic and busy, busy.

1 Marinate chicken wings for 15 minutes in a mixture of honey, hoisin sauce, water, salt, pepper, garlic, scallion and ginger.

2 Heat oven to 350 degrees. Place chicken wings on a baking sheet and bake for 30 minutes, brushing occasionally with marinade.

3 Turn oven to broil and broil chicken wings five more minutes. Turn wings every two minutes to avoid burning.

TO SERVE: Transfer chicken wings to a serving platter and serve hot or at room temperature.

NOTES:

15 chicken wings

1 tablespoon honey *or* syrup

4 tablespoons hoisin sauce

3 tablespoons warm water

¾ teaspoon salt

½ teaspoon black pepper

2 garlic cloves, *finely minced*

1 scallion, *finely minced*

1 slice fresh ginger, *minced*

ASPARAGUS SALAD [Sà Lách Măng Tây]

Serves 4 to 6

I call this salad my "lazy salad" since it requires very little time and effort. Asparagus Salad is a perfect light lunch by itself, a healthy, low-fat side dish to serve with any entrée.

1 Thoroughly wash and trim the asparagus, and cut into two-inch pieces. In a medium saucepan, bring water to a boil and cook asparagus for three minutes. In a colander, quickly rinse asparagus under cold running water and drain thoroughly.

2 Seed tomato and dice.

3 Heat olive oil over medium heat, add chopped scallions and stir-fry for a few seconds. Remove scallions from heat and set aside.

4 Toss all ingredients with Vinegar Salad Dressing (page 27). Chill until serving time.

TO SERVE: Toss just before serving to combine well and arrange on serving plates.

NOTES:

20 stalks fresh asparagus

1 medium tomato

1 teaspoon olive oil

2 scallions, *chopped*

2 tablespoons roasted, unsalted sesame seeds

¾ cup Vinegar Salad Dressing (page 27)

WATERCRESS TOPPED WITH BEEF AND ONION [Thịt Bò Trộn Xà Lách Son]

Serves 4 to 6

The first year I lived in Carlisle, Pennsylvania, I discovered a lake near a friend's home. To my delight, in spring, watercress grew in abundance along the banks! This was a priceless discovery, because you couldn't often find it in the grocery in those days. Every weekend we would pick the tender greens and serve them during the week as a nutritious part of our meals, fresh in a salad, cooked in clear soup, or in this dish.

1 Wash watercress thoroughly. Rinse in cold water and drain thoroughly. Arrange watercress and tomato slices on a large serving platter.

2 Heat olive oil in a nonstick sauté pan until hot. Brown garlic, then add chopped onion and stir until softened. Stir in beef, scallions and salt, and cook for about two minutes.

TO SERVE: Pour hot beef mixture over watercress and tomato on platter, drizzle with Vinegar Salad Dressing (page 27), sprinkle with freshly ground black pepper and serve immediately accompanied with Sweet and Sour Fish Sauce (page 24).

NOTES:

2 bunches watercress

1 medium tomato, *thinly sliced*

1 teaspoon olive oil

2 garlic cloves, *sliced*

½ medium onion, *thinly sliced*

1 cup tender beef steak, *thinly sliced*

2 scallions, *chopped*

1 cup Vinegar Salad Dressing (page 27)

¼ teaspoon salt

¼ teaspoon black pepper

Sweet and Sour Fish Sauce (page 24)

VIETNAMESE CHICKEN SALAD

[Gỏi Gà]

Serves 4 to 6

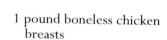

This recipe is very low in fat and has become a favorite dish with the clients that patronize my dressmaking business who are trying to perfect their figures. Clients report good results!

1 Put chicken breasts in a medium saucepan, with water to barely cover, bring to a boil, turn heat to simmer and cook for 15 minutes, or until chicken is cooked through. Cool and shred chicken into strips with your fingers.

2 In a large bowl, toss together the shredded cabbage and half of the salt. Set cabbage aside for 10 minutes. Rinse cabbage with cold water. Drain and dry.

3 Reserve some of the chicken, mint or cilantro, chile pepper, and sesame or peanuts to decorate serving dish. In a large bowl, toss together the remaining chicken, the shredded cabbage, the remaining salt, carrots, the remaining chicken, mint or cilantro and sesame or peanuts. Refrigerate until serving time.

4 Toss mixture with ½ cup Vinegar Salad Dressing (page 27) and three tablespoons Sweet and Sour Fish Sauce (page 24).

TO SERVE: Garnish with reserved chicken, mint or cilantro, chile pepper, sesame or peanuts. Pass the remaining Sweet and Sour Fish Sauce (page 24). Serve with shrimp paste chips or tortilla chips. Traditionally served wtih Chicken Rice Soup (page 53).

NOTES:

1 pound boneless chicken breasts

½ head small white cabbage, *shredded*

2 carrots, *shredded*

1 teaspoon salt

5 mint *or* cilantro sprigs, *minced*

1 red *or* green chile pepper, *sliced*

¼ cup roasted sesame seeds *or* crushed peanuts

½ cup Vinegar Salad Dressing (page 27)

1 cup Sweet and Sour Fish Sauce (page 24)

PAPAYA SHRIMP SALAD [Gỏi Đu Đủ]

Serves 4 to 6

Every summer, we went back to my father's hometown, which is sixty miles from Saigon. In this small town all the fruits and vegetables were harvested daily. It is impossible to beat the freshness and simplicity of produce grown on the spot. My sister often added fresh red chile peppers to her salad dressing...she likes it hot! A spicy dressing is perfect with this salad.

1 Cut the pork into 1-inch thick strips. In a medium saucepan, simmer the pork strips in water to barely cover for about 20 minutes, or until well done. Remove pork strips, reserving stock, and cool the strips before slicing them into thin pieces. In the same saucepan reheat stock with the shrimp and cook about five minutes. Drain shrimp and devein when cool enough. Set aside.

2 Peel papaya and divide into four. Finely shred papaya and carrots.

3 In a deep pan, cover papaya and carrots with cold water and salt. Set aside for 20 minutes, then rinse in cold water, drain and dry.

4 Add the red chile pepper to the Vinegar Salad Dressing (page 27) if you like—instant zip!

5 Reserve some of the pork, shrimp, cilantro, mint and peanuts for garnish. In a large bowl, toss together the shredded papaya and carrots, the remaining pork, shrimp, herbs and peanuts and pour on the salad dressing. Refrigerate until serving time.

6 Remove salad mixture from refrigerator, add three tablespoons of Sweet and Sour Fish Sauce and and toss again. Mound in the center of a shallow serving dish and garnish with reserved ingredients.

TO SERVE: Serve with shrimp paste chips or tortilla chips, Sweet and Sour Fish Sauce (page 24) and more thinly sliced red chile pepper.

¼ pound lean boneless pork

20 shrimp

1 medium green papaya

2 carrots

1 teaspoon salt

1 red chile pepper, *thinly sliced (optional)*

1 cup Vinegar Salad Dressing (page 27)

10 cilantro sprigs, *minced*

10 mint sprigs, *minced*

¼ cup peanuts, *crushed*

1 cup Sweet and Sour Fish Sauce (page 24)

shrimp paste chips *or* tortilla chips

SPAGHETTI SQUASH SHRIMP SALAD [Gỏi Tôm]

Serves 4 to 6

I had lived in America for several years before I discovered to my joy that spaghetti squash is a perfect substitute for papaya, particularly in salads.

1 In a deep pan, bring water to a boil. Divide spaghetti squash in half and cook 15 minutes. Cool and set aside.

2 Using a spoon, scoop out spaghetti squash. Fluff and separate strands with a fork. Shred carrots.

3 Follow instructions in the recipe for Papaya Shrimp Salad (opposite) beginning with Step **3**, substituting the squash for the papaya.

TO SERVE: Serve with shrimp paste chips or tortilla chips, the remaining Sweet and Sour Fish Sauce (page 24) and sliced red chile pepper.

NOTES:

1 spaghetti squash

¼ pound lean boneless pork

20 shrimps

2 carrots

1 teaspoon salt

1 red chile pepper, *thinly sliced (optional)*

1 cup Vinegar Salad Dressing (page 27)

10 cilantro sprigs, *minced*

10 mint sprigs, *minced*

¼ cup peanuts, *crushed*

1 cup Sweet and Sour Fish Sauce (page 24)

shrimp paste chips *or* tortilla chips

GINGER PINEAPPLE SALAD [Thơm Trộn Gừng]

Serves 4 to 6

This is a cooling salad or side dish—and a super slimming lunch.

1 In a large bowl, mix pineapple chunks, ginger, salt, sugar, cilantro and pepper. Thoroughly toss all ingredients together.

2 Refrigerate until serving time.

TO SERVE: This refreshing salad can be served alone or as an accompaniment to any entrée.

NOTES:

½ fresh pineapple,
  *yielding about 2 cups
  pineapple chunks*

1-inch piece ginger,
  peeled and finely minced

½ teaspoon salt

½ teaspoon sugar

10 cilantro sprigs,
  finely minced

½ red chile pepper,
  finely minced

SESAME SPINACH SALAD [Bó Xôi Trộn Mè]

Serves 4 to 6

After a long working day, I sometimes want only a very fast and easy dish such as this Sesame Spinach Salad. To make a complete meal, serve with shrimp, steak or any meat entrée.

2 pounds spinach

pinch of salt

1 teaspoon olive oil

2 scallions, *chopped*

¼ teaspoon salt

2 tablespoons roasted, unsalted sesame seeds

Vinegar Salad Dressing (page 27)

1 Wash the spinach very thoroughly. Discard the tough stems. Cut leaves in half. Bring water to a boil and add salt. Blanch spinach about one minute. Rinse in cold water and drain thoroughly.

2 Heat olive oil over medium heat, add chopped scallions and stir quickly. Remove scallions from heat and set aside.

3 In a mixing bowl, toss spinach, scallions, remaining salt and sesame seeds. Keep refrigerated until serving time.

4 Add four tablespoons Vinegar Salad Dressing (page 27). Toss to combine. Serve immediately.

NOTES:

LIME STEAK SALAD [Bò Tái Chanh]

Serves 4 as a main course or serves 6 as an appetizer

Lime Steak is similar to Italian carpaccio. Lime, or lemon, juice is used to cure the rare beef in both recipes. Lime Steak is a common bar food, like buffalo wings are here. My uncle frequently prepared this dish when his friends came to visit. Gathered around a small wooden table, they would talk for hours while drinking rice wine and snacking.

1 Slice beef into thin strips.

2 In a mixing bowl, toss together beef, sliced onion, salt, pepper, fish sauce, sugar, lime or lemon juice, red chile pepper, half the peanuts and culantro. Reserve remaining peanuts and a few herb sprigs for garnish.

3 Toss again before serving and garnish with ngo gai and peanuts.

TO SERVE: This is a spicy dish. Add more lime and red chile pepper, if you wish. Pass the Sweet and Sour Fish Sauce (page 24). This dish goes well with a glass of beer or wine.

1½ pounds of tender beef, *grilled, very rare (just seared on the grill)*

1 medium onion, *thinly sliced*

1 teaspoon salt

½ teaspoon freshly ground black pepper

3 tablespoons fish sauce

2 tablespoon sugar

6 tablespoons lime *or* lemon juice

1 fresh red chile pepper, *thinly sliced*

½ cup peanuts, *crushed*

15 culantro, ngo gai, sprigs, *or* fresh cilantro, *finely chopped*

Sweet and Sour Fish Sauce (page 24)

LIME CLAM SALAD [Hến Tái Chanh]

Serves 4 as a main course or serves 6 as an appetizer

In 1993, I came back to Vietnam for the first time after 18 years in the United States. I managed to find about half a dozen of my classmates from St. Paul Institution Francais. We gathered at a Hue restaurant and talked and laughed for hours. One of the dishes on the menu that evening, was my favorite, Lime Clam Salad, which is a variation of Lime Steak Salad.

1 In a nonstick pan, sauté the clams, with garlic and onion, until just cooked through, about two minutes. Remove from heat and cool.

2 Reserve some peanuts and culantro for garnish.

3 When clams have cooled, transfer to a large mixing bowl. Combine cooked clams with remaining ingredients, tossing to mix well.

TO SERVE: Serve immediately with crisp shrimp paste chips or tortilla chips accompanied with Sweet and Sour Fish Sauce (page 24).

NOTES:

1 pound shucked, fresh small clams

2 garlic cloves, *finely minced*

1 medium onion, *thinly sliced*

1 teaspoon salt

½ teaspoon freshly ground black pepper

3 tablespoons fish sauce

1 teaspoon sugar

6 tablespoons lime *or* lemon juice

1 fresh red chile pepper, *thinly sliced*

½ cup peanuts, *crushed*

15 culantro, ngo gai, *or* fresh cilantro sprigs, *finely chopped*

shrimp paste chips *or* tortilla chips

Sweet and Sour Fish Sauce (page 24)

Soups

CLEAR VEGETABLE SOUP [Canh Rau]

Serves 4 to 6

I have given this recipe to many customers in my 17 years in the fashion business. People want the recipe because it is an appetizing, light and low-fat soup…slimming and healthy! Use as many different vegetables as you like. This soup is quite filling.

1 If using shrimp, shell and devein. Use back of cleaver to smash shrimp, then finely mince to a paste. Mix in sugar, salt and pepper.

2 If using ground meat, mix in sugar, salt and pepper.

3 Wash and coarsely chop vegetables. Set aside.

4 In a medium soup pot, bring water to a boil, add shrimp paste or ground meat paste a teaspoon at a time. Skim foam until broth is clear. Add vegetables of your choice. Cook two minutes, then add fish sauce or salt.

TO SERVE: Transfer soup to a large bowl. Garnish soup with cilantro, scallions and an additional pinch of pepper.

10 shrimp *or* 1 cup of ground meat (pork, beef *or* turkey)

¼ teaspoon sugar

½ teaspoon salt

¼ teaspoon black pepper

4 cups vegetables (broccoli, watercress, cabbage, spinach—choose your favorites)

4 cups water

2 tablespoons fish sauce *or* ½ teaspoon salt

GARNISH:

5 cilantro sprigs, *finely chopped*

2 scallions, *thinly sliced*

pinch of black pepper

MUSTARD GREEN GINGER SOUP [Canh Cải Bẹ Xanh]

Serves 4 to 6

A spicy version of my Clear Vegetable Soup.

1 If using shrimp, shell and devein. Use back of cleaver to smash shrimp, then finely mince to a paste. Mix in sugar, salt and pepper.

2 If using ground meat, mix in sugar, salt and pepper.

3 In a medium soup pot, bring water to a boil. Add shrimp or ground meat mixture a teaspoon at a time. Skim foam until broth is clear. Add mustard greens and ginger. Cook five to eight minutes until greens are tender. Remove the lump of ginger. Add fish sauce or salt.

TO SERVE: Serve hot in large bowls garnished with cilantro, scallions and pepper.

NOTES:

10 shrimp *or* 1 cup of ground meat (pork, beef *or* turkey)

¼ teaspoon sugar

½ teaspoon salt

¼ teaspoon black pepper

4 cups water

2 pounds mustard greens, *well-washed and coarsely chopped*

1-inch piece of fresh ginger, *smashed*

2 tablespoons fish sauce *or* ½ teaspoon salt

GARNISH:

5 cilantro sprigs, *finely chopped*

2 scallions, *thinly sliced*

freshly ground black pepper

BUTTERNUT SQUASH SOUP [Canh Bí Rợ Nâú Tôm]

Serves 4 to 6

When I was in high school doing my final examinations, my aunt used to make this Butternut Squash Soup. She claimed that squash was brain food for a better memory. I loved her soup—and I passed the exams with distinction!

1 If using shrimp, shell and devein. Use back of cleaver to smash shrimp, then finely mince to a paste. Mix in sugar, salt and pepper.

2 If using ground meat, mix in sugar, salt and pepper.

3 In a medium soup pot, bring water to a boil. Add squash cubes. Cook eight to 10 minutes until squash is tender. Add shrimp or ground meat mixture a teaspoon at a time. Skim foam until broth is clear. Add fish sauce or salt.

TO SERVE: Serve in large bowls garnished with cilantro, scallions and pepper.

NOTES:

10 shrimp *or* 1 cup of ground meat (pork, beef *or* turkey)

¼ teaspoon sugar

½ teaspoon salt

¼ teaspoon black pepper

4 cups water

2 pound butternut squash, *peeled, seeded and cubed*

2 tablespoons fish sauce *or* ½ teaspoon salt

GARNISH:

5 cilantro sprigs, *finely chopped*

2 scallions, *thinly sliced*

freshly ground black pepper

CHICKEN RICE SOUP [Cháo Gà]

Serves 4 to 6

When I was a little girl, my mother always made me this soup when I was sick. Spiced with lots of black pepper and ginger, she would coax me to eat it while it was steaming hot. It always cured me! Was it the Chao Ga, my mother's tender loving care, or the wonderful combination?

1 Wash and drain rice thoroughly. Heat the oil in a frying pan and stir-fry rice and onion until rice turns white. Set aside.

2 In a soup pot, combine water, ginger, chicken and salt, and bring to a boil. Skim off the foam until clear and simmer until chicken is cooked through, about 20 minutes. Remove chicken from the pot and add rice and onion mixture. Simmer for 45 minutes.

3 Skin, debone and coarsely shred the chicken and return it to the soup. Before serving, add scallions and cilantro and sprinkle with black pepper.

TO SERVE: This soup can be served with Vietnamese Chicken Salad (page 41). If you prefer duck soup, substitute duck for the chicken in this recipe. Pass the Sweet and Sour Ginger Fish Sauce (page 24).

NOTES:

½ cup rice

1 tablespoon oil

1 onion, *coarsely chopped*

7 cups water

1-inch slice ginger, *smashed*

½ chicken *or* 4 chicken breasts

½ teaspoon salt

GARNISH:

2 scallions, *cut in 1-inch-long pieces*

5 sprigs cilantro, *finely chopped*

pinch of black pepper

Sweet and Sour Ginger Fish Sauce (page 24)

CHICKEN NOODLE SOUP [Phở Gà]

Serves 4 to 6

My husband said he could eat Pho every single day. Introduced from the North, it has become popular throughout Vietnam. When my husband and I were first married, we would stop by a pho restaurant for breakfast before going to work. I shall never forget the aroma coming from the huge soup pot. I always add an egg yolk to each bowl of soup to make it extra-special.

1 Broil onion and ginger until they look burned. Using back of cleaver, smash the ginger, and set aside.

2 Wash chicken bones, place in a large soup pot and add water to cover. Bring to a boil and immediately pour off this "first boiling" water and discard. This extra "boil-up" cleanses the bones and yields a clearer broth. Add another 12 cups of fresh water and again bring to a boil. Skim off foam. Add the broiled onion and ginger, star anise, salt and sugar. Over medium-low heat, simmer for 30 minutes.

3 Add chicken breasts and simmer until cooked through, about 20 minutes.

4 Remove chicken breasts from broth, skin and debone, cool and slice into ¼-inch strips. Strain broth, discard bones and solids.

5 Soak noodles in cold water for 10 minutes. Drain. In a soup pot bring two quarts fresh water to a boil. Add drained noodles and cook seven minutes at a rolling boil, stirring occasionally until noodles are tender.

6 Rinse noodles under cold running water and set aside.

TO SERVE: Divide noodles among four to six large individual serving bowls. Arrange chicken, scallions, onion and cilantro on top. Add one whole egg yolk to each serving bowl, if desired. Pour hot broth to cover noodles and serve immediately with garnishes and sauces.

BROTH:

1 small onion, *chopped*

1 2-inch stick ginger

2 pounds chicken bones

12 cups water

6 star anise

1 teaspoon salt

½ teaspoon sugar

1 pound chicken breasts

1 egg yolk per serving, *if desired*

NOODLES:

1 16-ounce package dry, flat rice noodles (pho)

GARNISH:

3 scallions, *thinly sliced*

1 large onion, *thinly sliced*

10 cilantro sprigs, *finely chopped*

1 cup bean sprouts

10 sprigs basil

10 sprigs fresh culantro

fresh red or green chile pepper, *thinly sliced*

ACCOMPANIMENTS:

lime *or* lemon quarters

fish sauce

hoisin sauce

hot chile sauce

BEEF NOODLE SOUP [Phở Bò]

Serves 4 to 6

This is a variation of the Pho Ga, Chicken Noodle Soup. Beef bones are used for the stock instead of chicken bones. The very thinly sliced beef is used instead of chicken.

1 Broil onion and ginger until they look burned. Using back of cleaver, smash the ginger and set aside.

2 Wash beef bones, place in a large soup pot and add water to cover. Bring to a boil and immediately pour off this "first-boiling" water and discard. Add another 12 cups of fresh water and again bring to a boil. Skim off foam. Add the broiled onion and ginger, star anise, salt and sugar. Over medium-low heat, simmer for 30 minutes.

3 Slice raw beef into thin strips and set aside.

4 Remove bones from broth and strain out vegetables and seasonings.

5 Soak noodles in cold water for 10 minutes. Drain. In a soup pot bring two quarts fresh water to a boil. Add drained noodles and cook seven minutes at a rolling boil, stirring occasionally until noodles are tender.

6 Rinse noodles under cold running water and set aside.

7 Return the broth to a boil over high heat.

BROTH:

1 small onion, *chopped*

1 2-inch stick ginger

2 pounds beef bones

12 cups water

6 star anise

1 teaspoon salt

1 teaspoon sugar

1 pound lean, tender beef

NOODLES:

1 16-ounce package dry, flat rice noodles (pho)

GARNISH:

3 scallions, *thinly sliced*

1 large onion, *thinly sliced*

10 cilantro sprigs, *finely chopped*

1 cup bean sprouts

10 sprigs basil

10 sprigs fresh culantro

fresh red or green chile pepper, *thinly sliced*

ACCOMPANIMENTS:

lime *or* lemon quarters

fish sauce

hoisin sauce

hot chile sauce

TO SERVE: Divide noodles among four to six large individual serving bowls. Arrange thinly sliced raw beef, scallions, onion and cilantro on top. Pour boiling hot broth to cover noodles and serve immediately. The boiling broth will cook the thin slices of beef. Pho is always accompanied by bean sprouts, basil leaves, culantro and chile pepper. Serve with lime and lemon quarters, fish sauce, hoisin sauce and hot chile sauce.

NOTES:

CHICKEN or SHRIMP PINEAPPLE SOUP [Canh Chua Thơm]

Serves 4 to 6

Light and fast to make, this soup is usually served with a salty fish or meat dish and a side dish of vegetables. Use either chicken breasts or shrimp.

1 In a small bowl, mix warm water and tamarind pulp. Mash tamarind with a small spoon to extract as much tamarind juice as possible. Set aside.

2 In a small soup pot, heat oil and sauté the minced garlic until brown. Stir in pineapple and sugar. Add four cups water and bring to a boil.

3 Add tamarind mixture, shrimp, tomato and fish sauce or salt. Skim off foam and simmer for five minutes.

TO SERVE: Garnish with scallions, rau om and sliced red chile pepper.

NOTES:

¼ cup warm water

1 tablespoon tamarind pulp

1 teaspoon oil

2 garlic cloves, *minced*

½ fresh pineapple, *cored and thinly sliced, or* 1 can sugar-free chunk pineapple

1 teaspoon sugar

4 cups water

10 medium shrimp, *shelled and deveined or* 2 large, boneless chicken breasts

1 tomato, *cut into eight pieces*

2 tablespoons fish sauce *or* ½ teaspoon salt

GARNISH:

1 scallion, *sliced*

5 sprigs rau om *or* culantro *or* cilantro

red chile pepper, *thinly sliced*

BEAN THREAD CHICKEN SOUP [Miến Gà]

Serves 4 to 6

This traditional soup, from the North of Vietnam, is a lighter version of Pho. Most Vietnamese eat it for breakfast. I prefer it for dinner, especially on a cold night.

1 Wash chicken bones and place in a large saucepan. Add water to cover and bring to a boil. Immediately drain the bones, discarding water. Add another 10 cups of fresh water and again bring to a boil. Skim off foam. Add salt and sugar. Over medium-low heat, simmer for 30 minutes. Add chicken breasts and simmer until cooked through.

2 Soak bean thread in cold water for 15 minutes. Drain, and cut bean thread into short segments.

3 Remove chicken breasts from broth. When cooled, debone and shred breast meat.

4 Strain bones out. Bring broth to a boil, then simmer about three minutes.

TO SERVE: Transfer bean thread into large individual serving bowls. Add shredded chicken, scallion and cilantro leaves. Pour sufficient hot broth to cover. Serve immediately. Add lime or lemon to taste.

NOTES:

CHICKEN STOCK:

2 pounds chicken bones

10 cups water

1 teaspoon salt

½ teaspoon sugar

½ pound chicken breasts

NOODLES:

5 ounces dry bean thread noodles

GARNISH:

2 scallions, *thinly sliced*

10 sprigs cilantro

lime *or* lemon quarters

ASPARAGUS CRAB SOUP [Súp Măng Tây]

Serves 6 to 8

To celebrate my 17th birthday, my mother and my aunts had a dinner party at our home. The night before, six of us sat around picking crab-meat from two bushels of cooked blue crabs to make this elegant soup. I loved the party!

1 Wash chicken bones and place them in a soup pot. Cover them with water and bring to a boil, drain immediately. Add another 10 cups of fresh water and bring to a boil again. Skim off the foam. Add salt and sugar. Simmer over medium-low heat for one hour. Strain and discard bones. Set broth aside for use in Step **3**.

2 Heat the oil in a frying pan and stir-fry the onion until soft. Add crabmeat and stir-fry about three minutes. Set aside.

3 Bring seven cups of broth to a boil. Gently stir in the onion, crabmeat, salt and sugar. Turn heat to low and skim foam until clear.

4 Mix the tapioca starch or cornstarch with one-fourth cup water in a small bowl. Pour slowly into broth, then drop in the cut asparagus spears. Using a teaspoon, add beaten egg to the soup a drop at a time. Add sugar, taste for seasoning and immediately turn off heat.

TO SERVE: Reheat soup and pour into small bowls. Sprinkle pepper and red vinegar, if using. Shredded chicken can be substituted for the crabmeat.

NOTES:

CORN CRAB SOUP [Súp Bắp Cua]

This is a variation of the Asparagus Crab Soup and is often served at wedding feasts in Vietnam.

For the Corn Crab Soup, substitute the kernels cut from four ears of fresh corn or two cups of canned corn for the asparagus in the previous recipe.

NOTES:

CHICKEN STOCK:

2 pounds chicken bones
 or pork bones

10 cups water

½ teaspoon salt

½ teaspoon sugar

1 teaspoon oil

½ onion, *chopped*

1 cup fresh backfin
 crabmeat

1 teaspoon salt

1 teaspoon sugar

1 tablespoon tapioca
 starch *or* cornstarch

¼ cup water

1 pound fresh asparagus,
 *cleaned, trimmed and cut
 in 1-inch pieces*

1 egg, *beaten*

1 teaspoon sugar

ground black pepper

red vinegar *(optional)*

CHARSIU PORK SOUP [Mì Xá Xíu]

Serves 6 to 8

I particularly like this Chinese-style soup because it brings back memories of a summer when I spent a long visit at the home of my parents' friend. I felt trapped inside the lovely French villa. I wasn't allowed to eat any food from the street vendors, something I loved to do at home. Every day I would hear enticing sounds coming from the other side of the garden wall. One such sound was the Chinese soup vendor, advertising his soup in the traditional way by clacking together two pieces of wood. I felt very sorry for myself. Fortunately for me, so did the maid, who slipped out and brought me a bowl of charsiu soup. It was a splendid treat! Charsiu pork is sometimes sold at Vietnamese grocery stores or carry out Chinese restaurants, but can easily prepared at home. Charsiu pork can be served as an entrée with rice or French bread or used in this traditional soup.

1 Divide pork into four pieces. In a large bowl, marinate pork in soy sauce, scallions, honey, red wine, salt, sugar and pepper, for five hours or overnight.

2 Meanwhile, make pork stock or use 10 cups chicken broth if you are pressed for time.

3 Wash pork bones and place in a large soup pot. Add water to cover and bring to a boil. Immediately drain the bones, discarding water. Add another 10 cups of fresh water and again bring to a boil. Skim off foam. Add whole onion, salt, sugar and oyster sauce. Simmer over medium-low heat for one hour.

4 Preheat oven to 375 degrees. Place marinated pork on a baking sheet. Bake for 45 minutes, turning occasionally to brown pork evenly. Cool and thinly slice meat. Set aside while you prepare noodles.

2 pounds lean boneless pork

3 tablespoons soy sauce

2 scallions, *finely sliced*

2 tablespoons honey

⅓ cup red wine

1 teaspoons salt

1½ teaspoons sugar

¼ teaspoon black pepper

PORK STOCK:

2 pounds pork bones

10 cups water

1 medium onion

1 teaspoon salt

1 teaspoon sugar

2 tablespoons oyster sauce

EGG NOODLES:

1 teaspoon oil

2 pounds egg noodles

1 tablespoon soy sauce

GARNISH:

16 sprigs watercress

15 cilantro sprigs, *finely chopped*

3 scallions, *thinly sliced*

freshly ground black pepper

red vinegar, *to taste*

5 Fill saucepan two-thirds full with water, add oil and bring to a boil. Drop each portion of egg noodles into boiling water for one minute. Stir with a fork or a pair of chopsticks. Remove noodles from saucepan and transfer to a colander. Repeat with the rest of noodles. Rinse noodles with cold water. Drain thoroughly.

6 Add soy sauce to egg noodles and toss well.

TO SERVE: Place a portion of noodles in each individual soup bowl. Arrange thinly sliced pork on top. Pour in sufficient stock to cover and garnish bowl with watercress, cilantro, scallions and pepper. Pass a small pitcher of red vinegar to add for individual taste.

CRAB TOMATO SOUP [Bún Riêu]

Serves 4 to 6

This seafood soup with fresh tomatoes is a northern Vietnamese favorite—made with their plentiful, but tiny, crabs.

1 In a small bowl, soak dry shrimp for 10 minutes

2 In a soup pot, cover bones with water, bring to a boil and simmer for five minutes. Drain and rinse pork bones. Add eight cups of fresh water, dried shrimp, salt and fish sauce, and bring to a boil. Simmer about 30 minutes, skimming occasionally.

3 Add tomatoes to soup pot. Simmer over medium heat for 10 minutes.

4 In a medium bowl, mix egg, crabmeat, ground pork, salt and pepper. Using a large spoon, carefully add mixture to soup, and continue to simmer until mixture rises to the surface.

5 Heat oil in a small saucepan and fry onion until brown. Scrape onion and oil into soup pot and remove from heat.

6 In a deep saucepan, bring water to a boil, add rice vermicelli, and stirring occasionally, cook for about five minutes. It should be clear white and soft. Rinse under running cold water, drain thoroughly and set aside.

TO SERVE: Divide cooked rice vermicelli among medium soup bowls. Pour soup over noodles and stir in fish sauce and ground red chile pepper to taste. Add a serving of Garden Salad (opposite) to each steaming bowl of soup.

NOTES:

½ cup dry shrimp

3 pounds pork bones

8 cups water

1½ tablespoons salt

1 tablespoon fish sauce

2 ripe medium tomatoes, *diced*

1 egg

½ pound fresh backfin *or* lump crabmeat

⅓ cup ground pork

pinch of salt and pepper

1 teaspoon oil

½ medium onion, *sliced*

RICE VERMICELLI (BUN):

8 cups water

1 pound package dry, rice vermicelli

fish sauce, *to taste*

ground red chile pepper, *to taste*

GARDEN SALAD [Rau Sống]

1 Strip leaves from herb sprigs and discard stems. Wash all vegetables thoroughly. Spin dry, and arrange herbs, lettuce, bean sprouts and lime quarters on a serving platter. Add a serving of salad to each steaming bowl of soup.

NOTES:

GARDEN SALAD:

10 cilantro sprigs

10 mint sprigs

10 basil sprigs

½ head lettuce, *shredded*

1 cup bean sprouts

1 lime, *quartered*

Main Dishes

GINGER CHICKEN [Gà Kho Gừng]

Serves 4

Ginger is considered a medicine and *an essential cooking ingredient in the Orient. Vietnamese believe it aids digestion and cures the common cold. Whenever I feel a cold coming on, I make ginger tea with several slices of fresh ginger in a small teapot with boiling hot water. It is so much better than drug store cold remedies!*

1 Marinate chicken in a mixture of honey, salt, pepper and cornstarch. Set aside for 15 minutes.

2 Heat the oil in a frying pan until hot. Sauté garlic until golden. Add marinated chicken and ginger, and stir until brown. Pour in water and fish sauce and simmer for 10 minutes. Add onions and scallions. Simmer about five minutes, stirring occasionally, until caramel colored.

TO SERVE: Sprinkle with black pepper to taste and serve hot with rice.

NOTES:

1 pound boneless chicken breasts, *cut into small cubes*

2 teaspoons honey

½ teaspoon salt

½ teaspoon black pepper

1 teaspoon cornstarch

1 tablespoon oil

2 cloves garlic, *finely minced*

1½-inch ginger, *finely chopped*

⅓ cup water

2 tablespoons fish sauce *or soy sauce*

½ small onion, *chopped*

3 scallions, *chopped*

freshly ground black pepper

SESAME CHICKEN IN ORANGE SAUCE [Gà Mè Sốt Cam]

Serves 4

This dish reminds me of my last year in high school, when my friends and I decided to practice making this dish. Imagine six teenagers in a small kitchen trying to light an old-fashioned charcoal stove. We joked and giggled through the whole experience. Despite all the mess we created in the kitchen, the dish turned out surprisingly well.

1 Toss the chicken with flour, salt, pepper and one-half teaspoon sugar. Set aside for 10 minutes.

2 In a small saucepan, mix orange juice, fish sauce, honey, one tablespoon sugar and cornstarch. Heat over medium heat until mixture thickens.

3 Heat the oil in a sauté pan until hot. Sauté garlic and onion until light brown. Add chicken, orange zest and sesame seeds. Stir-fry until golden brown.

4 Pour orange sauce over chicken, add orange slices and simmer over medium heat for two or three minutes.

TO SERVE: Place chicken in a serving dish, arranging the orange slices attractively on top. Serve with rice.

NOTES:

1 pound boneless chicken breasts, *cut into small cubes*

1 tablespoon flour

½ teaspoon salt

½ teaspoon black pepper

½ teaspoon sugar

1 cup orange juice

2 tablespoons fish sauce

1 tablespoon honey *or* 1 tablespoon sugar

½ teaspoon cornstarch

2 tablespoons oil

2 garlic cloves, *minced*

½ cup onion, *coarsely chopped*

zest from one fresh orange

2 tablespoons sesame seeds

1 orange, *sliced ¼-inch thick*

CASHEW CHICKEN [Gà Xào Hột Diêù]

Serves 4

Daughter Diana's favorite supper!

1 In a large bowl, mix chicken, flour, salt, pepper, sugar and two tablespoons oyster sauce. Set aside for 10 minutes.

2 Trim snow peas by pulling strings from both sides of pod. Wash and drain thoroughly.

3 Heat oil until hot in a large frying pan. Add garlic and onion, and stir-fry until fragrant, about one minute. Stir in chicken and cashews, and continue to stir-fry until light caramel brown, about 10 minutes. Add scallions and snow peas, and stir-fry for two minutes longer. Pour in remaining oyster sauce, stir quickly to coat ingredients, then remove immediately from heat.

TO SERVE: Transfer chicken to a serving dish and garnish with sprigs of cilantro. Sprinkle with ground black pepper and serve with rice.

1 pound boneless chicken breasts, *coarsely sliced*

1 tablespoon flour

1/3 teaspoon salt

1/2 teaspoon black pepper

2 teaspoons sugar

3 tablespoons oyster sauce

2 cups snow peas

2 tablespoons oil

2 garlic cloves, *minced*

1 small onion, *coarsely chopped*

1/2 cup cashews

3 scallions, *cut into 3-inch lengths*

4 sprigs cilantro for garnish

freshly ground black pepper, *to taste*

CHICKEN CURRY [Cà Ry Gà]

Serves 4

In Vietnam, we used to go to a restaurant owned by a family from India. This curry was their specialty. Often there would be two or three whole hot peppers in each bowl...a spicy, brow-mopping experience!

1 In a large bowl, thoroughly mix salt, red pepper, sugar, curry powder and tomato paste. Coat chicken with this mixture and marinate for 10 minutes.

2 Heat oil in a deep pot and stir-fry the garlic and lemongrass until fragrant. Add chicken and stir-fry about five minutes more. Pour water, milk and coconut milk into the pan, stir in sweet potato and simmer for 20 minutes.

TO SERVE: Indian curry is more often hot than not. Serve with French bread as we do in Vietnam or, if you prefer, serve this dish with rice.

2 teaspoons salt

½ teaspoon crushed red pepper

1 tablespoon sugar

3 tablespoons curry powder

3 tablespoons tomato paste

1 pound boneless chicken breasts, *cut into bite-sized pieces*

2 tablespoons oil

3 garlic cloves, *sliced*

1 stalk lemongrass, *finely chopped*

1 cup water

1 cup milk

1 cup coconut milk

1 medium sweet potato, *peeled and cut into large dice*

SPICY LEMONGRASS CHICKEN [Gà Xào Xả Ớt]

Serves 4

Lemongrass is often used in Vietnamese cooking and has become quite popular in American cooking—and in American herb gardens. Boneless, skinless chicken breasts are a great shortcut for busy cooks. I use them often for a fast supper for my hungry family.

1 Marinate chicken in a mixture of honey, salt, pepper and cornstarch for 15 minutes.

2 Heat the oil in the fry pan until hot and stir-fry garlic and onion until fragrant. Stir in lemongrass and red pepper, if using, and stir-fry one minute. Add marinated chicken and stir-fry until brown. Pour in water and fish or soy sauce, and simmer for 10 minutes, stirring occasionally until caramel brown. Sprinkle on scallions, toss and remove from heat.

TO SERVE: Place in a heated serving dish and sprinkle with ground black pepper.

NOTES:

1 pound boneless chicken breasts, *cut into small cubes*

2 teaspoons honey

½ teaspoon salt

½ teaspoon black pepper

1 teaspoon cornstarch

1 tablespoon oil

2 cloves garlic, *finely minced*

½ small onion, *chopped*

1 stalk lemongrass, *tender portion finely chopped*

1 hot red chile pepper, *minced (optional)*

⅓ cup water

2 tablespoons fish sauce *or* soy sauce

2 scallions, *finely sliced*

freshly ground black pepper, *to taste*

LEMON CHICKEN [Gà Nướng Chanh]

Serves 4

In Vietnam, lime is most often used instead of lemon. My mother would pick fresh limes and leaves from the tree that grew in our garden to flavor her cooking. When we had guests, she would barbecue this lemon chicken on skewers over the charcoal grill. Lemon chicken is a dish beloved by children. This tangy, honey-sweetened chicken can be served alone, with plain rice or rice vermicelli and a garden salad. It also makes a great sandwich between slices of French bread.

1 Marinate chicken in a mixture of honey, salt, pepper, sugar, garlic, oil, cornstarch, scallions, lemon or lime juice, fish sauce and oyster sauce. Set aside for 15 minutes. Add grated lemon or lime zest.

2 Thread marinated chicken onto skewers, leaving two inches free at each end and place on a baking sheet. Heat oven to 375 degrees and bake about 20 minutes until chicken is medium-rare. Turn oven to broil and broil chicken until brown. Do not overcook.

TO SERVE: Serve with rice vermicelli and Sweet and Sour Fish Sauce (page 24). Can also be served with rice. Garnish with bean sprouts, basil and mint.

NOTES:

1 pound boneless chicken, *cut into large cubes*

2 teaspoons honey

½ teaspoon salt

½ teaspoon black pepper

1 teaspoon sugar

2 cloves garlic, *finely minced*

1 teaspoon oil

½ teaspoon cornstarch

2 scallions, *finely sliced*

3 tablespoons lemon *or lime juice*

2 tablespoons fish sauce

1 tablespoon oyster sauce

2 tablespoons lemon *or lime zest, grated*

12 bamboo skewers, *soaked in water for at least 10 minutes*

Sweet and Sour Fish Sauce (page 24)

GARNISH:

bean sprouts

basil sprigs

mint sprigs

HONEY ROASTED QUAIL [Chim Cút Rôti]

Serves 4 to 6

Quail are considered "fancy" in Vietnam and served on special occasions such as a wedding.

1 Wash quail, drain and pat dry. Split birds in half.

2 In a large bowl, combine garlic, honey, sugar, pepper, salt, five-spice powder and fish sauce. Marinate birds in this mixture for one hour.

3 Preheat oven to 375 degrees. Place birds, skin side up, on a baking sheet, and bake for 15 minutes, turning after 10 minutes. Quail are ready when they turn golden brown and the leg bone yields to twisting.

4 Prepare Lime Salt and Pepper by mixing salt, pepper and lime juice.

TO SERVE: Arrange watercress on a large round plate. Top with roasted quail, Carrot Pickle (page 73) and lime slices and serve with Lime Salt and Pepper.

NOTES:

6 quail

3 garlic cloves, *minced*

1 tablespoon honey

2 teaspoons sugar

½ teaspoons black pepper

½ teaspoons salt

1 teaspoon five-spice powder

3 tablespoons fish sauce

LIME SALT AND PEPPER:

1 teaspoon salt

½ teaspoon black pepper

2 tablespoons lime *or* lemon juice

GARNISH:

1 bunch watercress

lime slices

Carrot Pickle (page 73)

BARBECUED PORK HANOI-STYLE [Bún Chả Hà Nội]

Serves 4

This Hanoi-style dish has become very popular in Saigon.

1 Marinate pork in honey, salt, pepper, garlic, oil, cornstarch, scallions, and fish sauce or oyster sauce. Set aside for 15 minutes.

2 Thread marinated pork onto skewers, leaving two inches free at each end. Place pork skewers on the grill, turning and brushing occasionally with the marinade, until they turn golden brown. You may also grill indoors under an oven broiler.

3 In a deep pot, bring water to a boil. Add rice vermicelli and stir gently until vermicelli is clear white and soft, about five minutes. Rinse under cold running water, drain thoroughly and set aside.

4 Prepare Garden Salad (page 63) and set aside.

5 Prepare Carrot Pickle (opposite).

TO SERVE: Strip barbecued pork from skewers and place in individual serving bowls. Top with Sweet and Sour Fish Sauce (page 24) and Carrot Pickle (opposite). Sprinkle crushed peanuts over all. Serve with white vermicelli, herbs and Garden Salad (page 63). This dish can also be served as an appetizer or with rice.

NOTES:

1 pound lean, boneless pork, *thinly sliced*

2 teaspoons honey

½ teaspoon salt

½ teaspoon freshly ground black pepper

2 cloves garlic, *finely minced*

1 teaspoon oil

½ teaspoon cornstarch

2 scallions, *finely sliced*

1 tablespoon fish sauce *or oyster sauce*

12 bamboo skewers, *soaked in water for at least 10 minutes*

½ pound rice vermicelli

Garden Salad (page 63)

Carrot Pickle (opposite)

Sweet and Sour Fish Sauce (page 24)

GARNISH:

crushed peanuts

minced herbs of your choice

CARROT PICKLE [Dồ Chua]

For most Vietnamese families, Carrot Pickle is a staple kept in their refrigerators. Carrot Pickle goes with any recipe that calls for Sweet and Sour Fish Sauce.

1 Mix carrot, sugar, water, vinegar and salt in a medium bowl. Toss well and set aside until serving time.

NOTES:

3 carrots, *shredded*

1 tablespoon sugar

¼ cup water

2 tablespoons vinegar

¼ teaspoon salt

MEATBALLS [Xíu Mại]

Serves 4

In Vietnam, these Meatballs, served with French bread and sprinkled with red vinegar, were my favorite breakfast dish.

1 In a large bowl, combine ground pork or beef, onion, scallions, oyster sauce, flour, sugar, salt and red pepper. Knead mixture until well-combined.

2 Form mixture into 12 meatballs and place in one layer in small oiled bowls in a steamer. Steam meatballs for 30 minutes.

TO SERVE: Transfer hot meatballs to a warm serving dish and top with Pineapple Tomato Sauce (page 27). These meatballs can be eaten as an entrée with rice or as a sandwich tucked into split French bread. Pass red vinegar and hot chile sauce.

1 pound ground pork
  or beef

1 small onion,
  finely chopped

2 scallions, *finely sliced*

1 tablespoon oyster sauce

2 tablespoons flour

1 teaspoon sugar

1 teaspoon salt

¼ teaspoon ground red
  pepper

1 teaspoon oil

Pineapple Tomato Sauce
  (page 27)

red vinegar

hot chile sauce

STUFFED TOMATOES [Cà Chua Dồn Thịt]
Serves 4

St. Paul Institution Francais, a French academy, was my boarding school for two years. We were served wonderful French food. I particularly loved these stuffed tomatoes. I would crush the tomato, mix it with the meat stuffing and eat it with a very crunchy baguette.

6 medium tomatoes

1 uncooked recipe of Meatballs mixture, (opposite)

Sweet and Sour Fish Sauce (page 24)

Pineapple Tomato Sauce (page 27)

1 Wash tomatoes and slice off their tops. Using a small sharp knife, core the tomatoes and scoop out the seeds. Set aside while preparing Meatballs recipe (opposite).

2 Fill each tomato to the top with meat filling.

3 Preheat oven to 375 degrees. Place tomatoes in an oiled baking dish and bake for about 30 minutes.

TO SERVE: Serve with Plain Rice (page 14). Pour Sweet and Sour Fish Sauce (page 24) or Pineapple Tomato Sauce (page 27) over tomatoes before serving.

SESAME SPARERIBS [Xường Nướng Mè]

Serves 4

This is my children's favorite appetizer. We gather around the table and munch on the honey-baked spareribs, hot from the oven. Served with plain rice, they can be a complete meal.

1 In a large bowl, mix together the scallions, sesame seeds, salt, fish sauce, honey, flour and sugar. Marinate the spareribs in this mixture for 15 minutes.

2 Preheat oven to 375 degrees. Bake spareribs for 20 minutes, turning occasionally. Turn oven setting to broil and broil ribs for five minutes, turning ribs frequently.

TO SERVE: Serve ribs hot as an appetizer, or with rice as an entrée. Be sure to accompany with Sweet and Sour Fish Sauce (page 24).

NOTES:

2 scallions, *finely sliced*

2 tablespoons sesame seeds

½ teaspoon salt

3 tablespoons fish sauce

2 tablespoons honey

1 teaspoon flour

1 teaspoon sugar

1½ pound spareribs (12)

Sweet and Sour Fish Sauce (page 24)

SALT AND PEPPER RIBS [Xường Ram Mặn]
Serves 4 to 6

*On my most recent trip to Vietnam, I visited Dalat, a resort town,
six hours from Saigon. We arrived late in the evening with everyone
tired and hungry. Our driver took us to a small restaurant for dinner.
We didn't have high expectations, the menu was simple. Surprisingly,
it was a wonderful meal. These Salt and Pepper Ribs were the highlight.
What makes this preparation so special is cooking the onions until
they are brown and the vigorous shaking of the cooking pan.*

1½–2 pounds baby back ribs (12–18)

½ teaspoon salt

½ teaspoon black pepper

½ teaspoon sugar

1 tablespoon oyster sauce

1 tablespoon oil

2 garlic cloves, *minced*

1 onion, *coarsely chopped*

1 Chop spareribs with a large heavy knife into two-inch lengths. In a
large bowl, marinate spareribs in a mixture of salt, pepper, sugar and
oyster sauce. Set aside for 15 minutes.

2 Heat oil in a large sauté pan until hot, and brown garlic and onion.
Add marinated spareribs, shaking the pan frequently. Stir-fry until
spareribs are browned and thoroughly cooked through, about 10 minutes.

TO SERVE: This dish is typically served with rice, a vegetable dish and
Clear Vegetable Soup (page 49).

NOTES:

SPICY LEMONGRASS PORK CHOPS [Xường Nướng Xả Ớt]

Serves 4

These pork chops were a great family favorite at a tiny restaurant near our home.

1 Combine fish sauce, oyster sauce, honey, salt, pepper, sugar and cornstarch in a large bowl. Marinate pork chops in this mixture for about 30 minutes.

2 Preheat oven to 375 degrees. Arrange pork chops on a baking sheet. Bake 20 minutes, turning occasionally.

3 Turn on broiler and broil on each side for five minutes. Watch carefully to avoid burning.

TO SERVE: Serve with Plain Rice (page 14), Tomato Rice (page 16), or Lemon Rice (page 16) and Sweet and Sour Fish Sauce (page 24).

NOTES:

3 tablespoons fish sauce

1 tablespoon oyster sauce

2 tablespoons honey

1 teaspoon salt

½ teaspoon freshly ground black pepper

1 teaspoon sugar

1 teaspoon cornstarch

1½ pound pork chops (4 pieces)

Sweet and Sour Fish Sauce (page 24) *(optional)*

STUFFED TOFU WITH SHRIMP AND PORK PASTE [Đậu Hũ Dồn Thịt]

Serves 4

I often watched my aunt making this dish. She managed to stuff the meat neatly inside the tofu without breaking it. The trick is to be very gentle and slow—and practice!

1 Drain tofu and slice into eight pieces measuring roughly 2" x 1½".

2 Using the back of a knife, smash shrimp, then mince finely to form a paste. Transfer to a medium bowl and thoroughly knead together the shrimp paste, pork, cornstarch, salt, pepper and sugar.

3 Slice tofu pieces almost in two and very gently stuff the cavity with a tablespoon of shrimp and pork paste. Repeat with remaining tofu and filling.

4 Heat oil in a nonstick frying pan until hot and carefully add stuffed tofu. Turn heat to medium and cook tofu, turning occasionally to insure an even golden brown color.

5 Remove tofu from oil and place on a paper towel-covered plate to absorb excess oil.

TO SERVE: Arrange tofu on a round plate and drizzle with Pineapple Tomato Sauce (page 27) or Sweet and Sour Fish Sauce (page 24).

NOTES:

1 4" x 6" cake hard tofu

10 shrimp, *shelled and deveined*

⅓ cup ground pork

½ teaspoon cornstarch

¼ teaspoon salt

¼ teaspoon black pepper

¼ teaspoon sugar

¼ cup oil

Pineapple Tomato Sauce (page 27)

Sweet and Sour Fish Sauce (page 24)

BEEF STEW VIETNAMESE STYLE [Bò Kho]

Serves 4

Beef stew was served with flat noodles almost always at breakfast time in Vietnam. If you ate in a restaurant, you would be served French bread alongside. For breakfast on the run, it would be served inside hollowed-out sections of French bread.

1 In a large bowl, mix together five-spice powder, curry powder, red pepper flakes, salt, tomato paste and oyster sauce. Marinate beef in this mixture for 15 minutes.

2 Heat oil in a large soup pot and stir-fry garlic and onion until browned. Stir in marinated beef and continue to stir-fry over medium heat for about 10 minutes. Pour in water and bring to a boil. Use a ladle to skim foam. Add carrots and lemongrass, and simmer stew over medium heat until beef chunks are tender—approximately one hour.

3 Meanwhile cook noodles in boiling water for five minutes, or until white and soft. Rinse and drain.

½ teaspoon five-spice powder

¼ teaspoon curry powder

½ teaspoon dried, crushed red pepper flakes *or* ground red pepper

2 teaspoon salt

2 tablespoons tomato paste

2 tablespoon oyster sauce

1½ pounds lean stew beef cubes

2 tablespoons oil

3 garlic cloves, *minced*

1 medium onion, *coarsely chopped*

5 cups water

5 carrots, *coarsely chopped*

1 stalk lemongrass, *stripped of outer leaves, cut in half and smashed*

1 pound flat rice noodles

TO SERVE: Serve stew with flat rice noodles and/or French bread. Garnish with basil and onion. Pass lime or lemon quarters and hoisin sauce.

NOTES:

GARNISH:

5 sprigs basil

½ onion, *thinly sliced*

lime *or* lemon quarters, *to taste*

hoisin sauce

SHAKING STEAK AND ONION [Bò Lúc Lắc]

Serves 4

*Another "miracle dish" so perfect for busy days and a hungry family…
very fast and easy steak! It's always pleasing to my two Vietnamese-
American children, and still capturing the familiar flavors of Vietnam
for my husband and me. You must use very tender steak.*

1 Mix together salt, pepper, sugar and oyster sauce. Stir in steak cubes
and marinate for 10 minutes.

2 Heat oil in a nonstick frying pan until hot, and stir-fry garlic and onion
until golden brown. Stir in steak cubes and continue to cook, shaking
frying pan occasionally, until steak is cooked to your taste.

TO SERVE: This dish is delicious served with fresh watercress, Sesame
Spinach Salad (page 45), Asparagus Salad (page 39) and Plain Rice (page
14) or Tomato Rice (page 16). I also like to serve some Lime Salt and
Pepper (page 71) with Shaking Steak.

NOTES:

½ teaspoon salt

½ teaspoon black pepper

¼ teaspoon sugar

1 tablespoon oyster sauce
   (optional)

1½ pounds of the
   tenderest cuts of beef
   steak, *cut into 1-inch
   cubes*

2 tablespoons oil

3 garlic cloves,
   thinly sliced

1 medium onion,
   coarsely chopped

Lime Salt and Pepper
   (page 71)

BEEF MEATBALLS [Chả Đùm]

Serves 4

In Saigon, there was a restaurant that served only beef dishes. It was called "Bo 7 Mon" meaning seven traditional beef courses. Selections included the favorite Beef Meatballs; Lime Steak; Grapeleaves Beef; Beef Fondue; Lemongrass Beef on Skewers; Shaking Steak; and Beef Soup.

1 In a medium bowl, soak bean thread in warm water for five minutes. Drain and cut into two-inch lengths.

2 In a large mixing bowl, knead together bean thread noodles, ground beef, salt, pepper, sugar, oyster sauce, flour, garlic, onion and oil. Set aside for 10 minutes.

3 Using your hands, make 10 meatballs, about two inches in diameter. Place them in a steamer over boiling water, and steam them for 25 minutes.

TO SERVE: Traditionally these meatballs are served with toasted sesame rice papers. Tortilla chips are a fine substitute or, if you wish, rice.

NOTES:

1 cup bean thread noodles

1½ pounds lean ground beef

1 teaspoon salt

1 teaspoon freshly ground black pepper

1¼ teaspoons sugar

1 tablespoon oyster sauce

2 tablespoons flour

3 garlic cloves, *minced*

1 medium onion, *chopped*

1 teaspoon oil

LEMONGRASS GROUND BEEF ON SKEWERS [Bò Nướng Xả]

Serves 4

My favorite after-school snack was Lemongrass Beef from the street vendors, grilled to perfection on a small charcoal brazier. Served by themselves, or with hoisin sauce and red chile sauce, they were delicious eaten on the spot, or tucked into a sandwich to "take along."

1 Using a mini food processor, finely mince lemongrass, onion and garlic.

2 In a large mixing bowl, knead together lemongrass mixture, ground beef, salt, pepper, sugar, oyster sauce, cornstarch, oil and scallions. Set aside for 15 minutes.

3 Make 12 meatballs approximately 1¾ inches in diameter. Thread them onto the skewers, leaving two inches free at each end. Oil your hands and gently squeeze meatballs along the skewer to form a sausage six inches long. Place beef skewers on the grill, and turn occasionally until they are a rich golden brown. You may also grill indoors under an oven broiler.

TO SERVE: These meatballs can be served as an appetizer with hoisin sauce and red chile sauce. Lemongrass Ground Beef would make a great entrée with Plain Rice (page 14) or Tomato Rice (page 16)—or pop them inside split French bread for a fast, portable lunch—and pass the Spicy Hoisin Sauce (page 27)

NOTES:

½ cup lemongrass, *finely minced*

1 medium onion, *chopped*

2 garlic cloves, *finely minced*

1½ pounds lean ground beef

1 teaspoon salt

½ teaspoon black pepper

1 teaspoon sugar

1 tablespoon oyster sauce

1 tablespoon cornstarch

1 teaspoon oil

2 scallions, *finely sliced*

12 bamboo skewers, *soaked in water for at least 10 minutes*

Spicy Hoisin Sauce (page 27)

GRAPE LEAF BEEF [Bò Cuốn Lá Nho]

Serves 4

Using the recipe for Lemongrass Ground Beef on Skewers, wrap the beef mixture in grapes leaves, which will give this dish an intriguing and unique flavor.

1 Place 1½ tablespoons of filling on each grape leaf one inch from the edge nearest you. Form a two-inch-long sausage. Fold inward both sides of leaf, and pressing down the mixture, fold over top of leaf and roll up. Repeat with remaining beef mixture.

2 Thread three rolls on each bamboo skewer. Barbecue beef skewers over hot coals or in a 400 degree oven, turning frequently for approximately 10 minutes until cooked through.

TO SERVE: Serve with Sweet and Sour Fish Sauce (page 24) as an appetizer, or with rice noodles as an entrée.

NOTES:

1 jar grapes leaves, *rinsed and spread out*

Lemongrass Ground Beef on Skewers recipe (page 85)

12 bamboo skewers, *soaked in water for at least 10 minutes*

Sweet and Sour Fish Sauce (page 24)

GRILLED SESAME BEEF [Bò Nướng Mè]

Serves 4

I often stopped for a snack at a little restaurant on my way to music school. This was the quickest dish, so I had enough time to savor the sesame beef with rice and Honey Sauce—and still make it to class on time. It's ideal for a picnic.

1 Marinate beef in a mixture of honey, salt, pepper, sugar, oyster sauce, garlic, cornstarch, sesame seeds and oil for 15 minutes.

2 Thread the marinated beef onto the skewers, leaving two inches free at each end. Set all the beef skewers on a baking sheet.

3 Place beef skewers on the grill, and turn occasionally until they are a rich golden brown, about three minutes on each side. You may also grill indoors under an oven broiler. Do not overcook.

TO SERVE: Serve as an appetizer with Honey Sauce (page 26) or as an entrée with rice and Sweet and Sour Fish Sauce (page 24). Grilled Sesame Beef also makes a great sandwich on French bread.

NOTES:

1 pound thinly sliced beef

2 teaspoons honey

½ teaspoon salt

½ teaspoon black pepper

1 teaspoon sugar

2 teaspoons oyster sauce

2 garlic cloves, *finely minced*

½ teaspoon cornstarch

¼ cup sesame seeds, *roasted*

1 teaspoon oil

12 bamboo skewers, *soaked in water for at least 10 minutes*

Honey Sauce (page 26)

Sweet and Sour Fish Sauce (Page 24)

CARAMEL SHRIMP [Tôm Rim]
Serves 4 to 6

The touch of dark sweetness adds a dramatic undertone to this savory shrimp. We love it on a cold winter evening.

1 Peel and devein shrimp. In a glass bowl add the oyster sauce, salt, pepper and flour to the shrimp. Marinate for five to 10 minutes.

2 Heat oil and sauté garlic until golden brown. Add shrimp and cook until they begin to turn pink. Add water and sugar, and simmer over medium heat for three minutes. Add scallions and onion, and stir-fry quickly until just cooked, about two minutes. Add red chile pepper… if you like the hot flavor. Sprinkle with freshly ground black pepper and squeeze the fresh lime over all.

TO SERVE: Garnish with fresh cilantro and serve immediately with lots of rice, a vegetable side dish or salad and Clear Vegetable Soup (page 49).

1½ pounds shrimp

2 tablespoons oyster sauce

½ teaspoon salt

½ teaspoon red pepper

½ teaspoon flour

3 tablespoons oil

3 cloves garlic, *minced*

½ cup water

2 tablespoons sugar

4 scallions, *white portion chopped*

1 small onion, *coarsely chopped*

1 fresh red chile pepper, *thinly sliced (optional)*

freshly ground black pepper

1 fresh lime

sprigs of fresh cilantro for garnish

SHRIMP IN GARLIC SAUCE [Tôm Sốt Tỏi]

Serves 4

Some days, feeling naughty, I make my version of a shrimp cocktail to enjoy all by myself. It is quick and delicious, so don't wait until you're in a bad mood to try it!

1 Rinse shrimp well and drain.

2 Melt butter over medium heat and stir-fry garlic until fragrant. Stir in shrimp, vinegar, water, salt and sugar. Cook, stirring gently for three to five minutes until shrimp turn pink and are just cooked through. Make sure shrimp are well coated with sauce.

TO SERVE: Eat shrimp, shells and all, or peeled, according to individual taste. Red wine or cold beer would complete the treat.

NOTES:

1–1½ pound medium shrimp, unpeeled

2 tablespoons butter

5 garlic cloves, *minced*

¼ cup white vinegar

¼ cup water

¼ teaspoon salt

¼ teaspoon sugar

GINGER AND SCALLION SHRIMP [Tôm Xào Gừng Hành]

Serves 4

When I moved to Washington, D.C., after a year in Carlisle, Pennsylvania, friends took us to dinner at one of the local Vietnamese restaurants for our first "American" shrimp. It was the best! I now prepare it often—fast and handy.

1 Devein shrimp, using a sharp steak knife to cut through the shell. Do not remove shell. Marinate shrimp in a mixture of oyster sauce, flour, salt and pepper.

2 Heat the oil in a frying pan until hot, and stir-fry garlic, ginger and onion until brown. Stir in shrimp and scallions and continue to stir-fry for three to five minutes or until shrimp are pink and cooked through.

TO SERVE: This popular dish is served with Plain Rice (page 14).

NOTES:

24 medium shrimp, unpeeled

1 teaspoon oyster sauce

2 teaspoons flour

½ teaspoon salt

½ teaspoon black pepper

1 tablespoon oil

3 garlic cloves, *minced*

1-inch piece ginger, *peeled and thinly sliced*

½ small onion, *chopped*

4 scallions, *cut in 1-inch pieces*

BAKED SALMON WITH GINGER AND SCALLION [Cá Nướng Gừng Hành]

Serves 4

In Vietnam we didn't have refrigeration at home. Every morning we went to the market to buy fresh fish. We selected the fish from a large tank. The vendor would clean it on the spot.

1 Rinse salmon fillets with cold water. Pat dry with paper towels.

2 Marinate salmon in a mixture of salt, pepper, oyster sauce, oil and ginger for 10 minutes.

3 Meanwhile preheat oven to 375 degrees.

4 Wrap salmon fillets tightly in heavy-duty aluminum foil and place on a baking sheet. Bake for 20 minutes.

5 Prepare the Scallion Sauté by heating oil over medium heat and stir-frying scallions and onion for two minutes. Remove from heat and set aside until serving time.

TO SERVE: Transfer salmon to a serving dish and pour the Scallion Sauté over the fish. Garnish with crushed peanuts, if using. This dish can be served with your choice of white rice, Lemon Rice (page 16) or with rice papers, accompanied by Garden Salad (page 63) and Sweet and Sour Fish Sauce (page 24).

NOTES:

1½ pounds salmon fillets
   or salmon steaks

¼ teaspoon salt

¼ teaspoon black pepper

1 tablespoon oyster sauce

1 teaspoon oil

1-inch piece ginger,
   peeled and thinly sliced

SCALLION SAUTÉ:

1 tablespoon oil

3 scallions, finely sliced

½ medium onion, *sliced*

1 tablespoon peanuts,
   *crushed for garnish
   (optional)*

Sweet and Sour Fish
   Sauce (page 24)

FRIED FLOUNDER IN GINGER SWEET AND SOUR FISH SAUCE

[Cá Chiên Dầm Nước Mắm]

Serves 4

A dramatic dish! If flounder is not available use sea bass, rockfish, blue fish, or snapper.

1 Wash fish, inside and out with salted water. Drain and dry.

2 Using a sharp knife, make shallow diagonal slashes on both surfaces of fish.

3 Mix flour, garlic, salt and pepper, and coat fish evenly on both sides.

4 In a nonstick frying pan, heat oil over medium heat. Gently slide fish into hot oil and fry until golden brown, turning once, until the meat is bright white and flakes easily.

5 Remove fish from oil and place on paper towel to drain.

TO SERVE: Place fish on a serving platter and garnish with watercress or lettuce. Traditionally, this dish is accompanied by a vegetable dish, such as Sesame Watercress (page 101) or Sesame Spinach Salad (page 45) and rice. Serve with Sweet and Sour Fish Sauce (page 24) or Sweet and Sour Ginger Fish Sauce (page 24) .

NOTES:

1 2-pound flounder, *split, cleaned and scaled, but with head and tail intact*

3 tablespoons all-purpose flour

2 garlic cloves, *finely minced*

¼ teaspoon salt

¼ teaspoon black pepper

2 tablespoons oil

watercress *or* lettuce leaves for garnish

Sweet and Sour Fish Sauce (page 24) *or* Sweet and Sour Ginger Fish Sauce (page 24)

LEMONGRASS FISH [Cá Chiên Ướp Xả]

Serve 3 to 4

This is a favorite dish in the southern Vietnamese oceanside resorts.

1 Clean salmon steaks. Using a sharp knife, make shallow, diagonal slashes on both surfaces of the salmon.

2 Marinate fish in a mixture of lemongrass, salt, black pepper, chile pepper and sugar for 10 minutes.

3 Heat oil in a nonstick skillet and sauté fish until golden brown, turning once.

TO SERVE: This fish is best served with rice, a vegetable dish or a salad, accompanied by a bowl of Clear Vegetable Soup (page 49).

NOTES:

1 pound salmon steaks

1 stalk lemongrass,
    finely minced

1 teaspoon salt

½ teaspoon freshly
    ground black pepper

½ fresh red chile pepper,
    finely minced

¼ cup sugar

2 tablespoons oil

VIETNAMESE FISH CAKES [Chả Cá Thià Là]

Serves 6 as an appetizer or 3 as a main course

These fish cakes feature red pepper and dill and are traditional in the northern regions of Vietnam. Fish paste is available frozen in Vietnamese or Thai markets...or make your own in a food processor: grind one-half pound boneless, fresh, white-fleshed fish fillet, washed and dried well with paper towels.

1 In a large bowl, combine fish paste, salt (omit the salt if you purchased *seasoned* fish paste), peppers, sugar, chopped dill, onion, scallions and cornstarch. Knead until paste is smooth.

2 Heat oil in a nonstick sauté pan over medium heat. Using two lightly oiled spoons, form paste into balls. Gently put fish balls in hot oil and flatten fish balls into round circles. Fry until golden brown. Drain on paper towels. Make small cakes to serve as appetizers and larger cakes to serve as a main course.

TO SERVE: As appetizers, accompany with Honey Sauce (page 26). As larger cakes, accompany with Sweet and Sour Fish Sauce (page 24) and Tomato Rice (page 16).

NOTES:

½ pound unseasoned fish paste

½ teaspoon salt

½ teaspoon black pepper

¼ teaspoon dry red chile pepper

1 teaspoon sugar

½ cup fresh dill, *finely chopped*

1 medium onion, red *or* white, *minced*

2 scallions, *thinly sliced*

1 tablespoon cornstarch

1 cup oil

Honey Sauce (page 26) *or* Sweet and Sour Fish Sauce (page 24)

CRAB CAKES [Chả Cua]
Serves 4

Crab cakes were my mother's specialty. In Vietnam, the crabmeat was freshly picked from blue crab. In the United States, choose fresh backfin or lump crabmeat.

1 Pick over crabmeat to remove any pieces of shell. In a large bowl, thoroughly mix crabmeat, salt, pepper, sugar, cornstarch, onion and eggs.

2 Heat oil in a nonstick sauté pan until hot, and using a large spoon, add a scoop of the crab mixture and flatten to form a round cake. Sauté until golden brown over medium heat. Remove crab cakes and place on a paper towel to drain.

TO SERVE: Serve piping hot with Plain Rice (page 14) or Tomato Rice (page 16) and Sweet and Sour Fish Sauce (page 24) or as a sandwich on French bread. Make smaller, bite-sized cakes to serve as an appetizer.

NOTES:

1 pound backfin *or* lump crabmeat

½ teaspoon salt

½ teaspoon black pepper

¼ teaspoon sugar

1 teaspoon cornstarch

1 small red *or* white onion, *finely chopped*

2 eggs, *lightly beaten*

1 tablespoon oil

Sweet and Sour Fish Sauce (page 24)

CRABS IN BEER [Cua Hấp Bia]

Serves 4 to 6

In Vietnam a beer called Beer 33 is the most popular (see photo, page 83), and Vietnamese prefer it served over ice. A number of foreign companies also produce beer in Vietnam and many more brands are imported.

1 Wash crabs thoroughly.

2 Place crabs in a large pot and pour in the vinegar, beer, water, salt and sugar.

3 Tightly cover pot and bring to a boil. Cook crabs over medium heat for 15 minutes until rosy red.

TO SERVE: Arrange crabs on a large warmed serving platter. Serve with Lime Salt and Pepper (page 71) and icy cold beer to drink.

NOTES:

2 dozen fresh, live, blue crabs

½ cup cider vinegar

2 12-ounce cans beer

1 cup water

½ teaspoon salt

½ teaspoon sugar

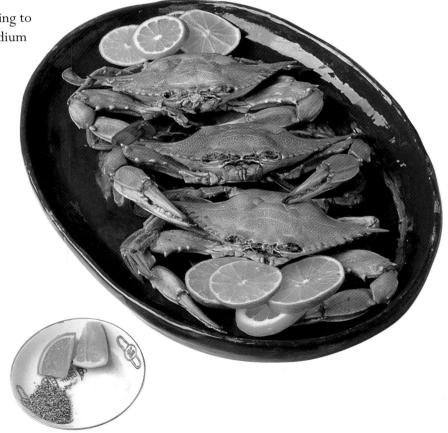

CLAMS or MUSSELS TOPPED WITH SCALLION OIL [Nghêu Xối Mở Hành]
Serves 4

The Vietnamese version of Clams Casino—but even better!

1 Using a stiff brush, scrub shellfish thoroughly under cold running water.

2 Preheat oven to 375 degrees. Place shellfish on a baking sheet and bake until shells open, about 10 minutes.

3 While clams or mussels are baking, heat oil in a small saucepan, stir in garlic and sauté until fragrant. Quickly toss in scallions, salt, sugar and pepper, stir once and promptly remove from heat. Set aside.

4 Remove top shell of each clam or mussel and dress with sautéed scallion mixture.

TO SERVE: Serve hot with a glass of red wine, if you wish.

NOTES:

2 dozen medium clams *or* large mussels

1 tablespoon oil

2 garlic cloves, *finely minced*

3 scallions, *finely sliced*

¼ teaspoon salt

¼ teaspoon sugar

¼ teaspoon freshly ground black pepper

VIETNAMESE CREPES [Bánh Xèo]

Serves 5

My high school friends and I loved to wander around one of the best markets in Vietnam, the famous Ben Thanh market in Saigon. It is filled with food vendors featuring many traditional Vietnamese delicacies…a tasting heaven! Our forays usually ended with the whole gang crowded around a little table feasting on these crispy crepes—Saigon pancakes—piping hot, straight from the vendor's wok.

1 Place pork in a saucepan, cover with water and bring to a boil. Simmer until well-cooked, about 20 minutes. Allow to cool, then thinly slice pork into thin ¼-inch strips.

2 Shell and devein shrimp and slice each one in half.

3 Wash and thoroughly drain the cilantro, basil, mint and lettuce. Set aside.

4 In a large bowl, make a batter with the flours, water, coconut milk, curry powder, sugar, salt and scallion, stirring well.

5 Divide sliced pork, shrimp, onion and bean sprouts into five equal portions.

6 Heat one tablespoon oil in a nonstick frying pan until very hot. Fry one portion of pork, shrimp and onion for barely a minute. Pour in one-half cup of batter, shaking the pan to coat the entire bottom evenly. Put one portion of bean sprouts in the center. Cover tightly. Turn the heat down to medium and fry crepe for three minutes. Loosen crepe, and using a spatula, fold crepe in half and transfer to a serving platter. Make four more crepes with the remaining ingredients. Crepes should be delicate and lightly crisp.

½ pound lean, boneless pork

20 medium shrimp

10 cilantro sprigs

10 basil sprigs

10 mint sprigs

10 leaves romaine lettuce

2 cups rice flour

½ cup self rising flour

2½ cups water

1 cup coconut milk *or* milk

½ teaspoon curry powder

1 teaspoon sugar

½ teaspoon salt

1 scallion, *chopped*

1 medium onion, *chopped coarsely*

3 cups bean sprouts

5 tablespoons olive oil

Sweet and Sour Fish Sauce (page 24)

TO SERVE: Serve these crepes hot and with individual bowls of sauce.
Do not cover crepes or stack them, or they will lose their crispness.
The traditional way to eat this crepe is to place it on a lettuce leaf, along
with a sprig or two of cilantro, basil and mint, roll it up and dip it in
Sweet and Sour Fish Sauce (page 24).

NOTES:

VIETNAMESE LOMEIN [Mì Xào]

Serves 4

If you like, add sautéed shrimp (or chicken) to this vegetarian dish as I have in the photograph below.

1 Fill a saucepan two-thirds full with water, add oil and bring to a boil. Add noodles and cook one minute, stirring with a fork. Tip noodles into a colander and rinse with cold water. Drain thoroughly. Toss noodles with soy sauce. Set aside.

2 If using dried mushrooms, soak in warm water for two hours or overnight. Cut off hard stems and discard. Slice mushrooms.

3 Heat oil in a large frying pan and stir-fry onion until fragrant. Stir in mushrooms, scallions, carrot, broccoli, snow peas, salt, pepper and sugar, and stir-fry two minutes. Stir in oyster sauce and remove from heat.

TO SERVE: Place noodles on warmed platter and top with vegetables. Garnish with cilantro. Serve with Sweet and Sour Soy Sauce (page 25).

EGG NOODLES:

1 teaspoon oil

1 pound egg noodles

1 tablespoon soy sauce

VEGETABLES:

5 dried black Chinese mushrooms *or* 6 fresh white mushrooms, *coarsely cut*

2 tablespoons oil

1 small onion, *chopped*

3 scallions, *chopped*

1 carrot, *thinly sliced*

1 cup broccoli, *coarsely chopped*

1 cup snow peas, *coarsely cut*

½ teaspoon salt

½ teaspoon black pepper

¼ teaspoon sugar

1 tablespoon oyster sauce *or* vegetarian oyster sauce

5 cilantro sprigs for garnish

Sweet and Sour Soy Sauce (page 25)

SESAME WATERCRESS [Rau Sốt Mỡ Hành]

Serves 4 to 6

Sometimes after a long working day, I need this fast and easy dish. The addition of shrimp or beef to this flavorful vegetable dish makes a complete meal. Various Asian cuisines favor specific greens and cabbage vegetables. The use of spinach suggests a Korean influence— watercress is more traditionally Vietnamese. Although Vietnam cooking included cauliflower in many dishes, I had never eaten broccoli until I came to the United States.

1 Wash watercress leaves thoroughly and discard tough stems. Cut leaves in two. Bring water to a boil, add salt, and blanch watercress about one minute. Rinse in cold water and press down on leaves to expel water.

2 Heat olive oil over medium heat, add scallions and sauté for 30 seconds. Remove scallions from heat and set aside.

3 In a mixing bowl, toss watercress, scallion oil, remaining salt and sesame seeds. Keep refrigerated until serving time.

TO SERVE: Sweet and Sour Fish Sauce (page 24) or Vinegar Salad Dressing (page 27) will give the Sesame Watercress extra flavor. If serving this dish to accompany Western entrées, use your favorite salad dressing.

NOTES:

2 pounds watercress
 or spinach

pinch of salt

1 teaspoon olive oil

2 scallions, *chopped*

¼ teaspoon salt

2 tablespoons roasted,
 unsalted sesame seeds

Sweet and Sour Fish
 Sauce (page 24) *or*
 Vinegar Salad Dressing
 (page 27)

STEAMED TOFU WITH SCALLION SAUCE [Đậu Hủ Hấp Mở Hành]

Serves 4 to 6

My aunt is a Buddhist vegetarian. Tofu supplies her daily protein needs. After years of sampling her tofu recipes, this one is my hands-down favorite...simple to prepare, vegetarian, low-fat and nutritious.

1 Divide each tofu into eight pieces and place in a shallow bowl. Thoroughly combine the fish sauce, honey and warm water until honey is emulsified.

2 Pour mixture over tofu, place bowl in a steamer and steam for about 10 minutes. You may heat the tofu in a microwave oven if you wish. Heat for two to three minutes on high, until steaming hot.

3 Heat oil in a small frying pan and stir-fry chopped scallions until soft.

TO SERVE: Garnish tofu and sauce with the chopped scallions and serve piping hot.

NOTES:

3 4" x 6" pieces hard tofu

2 tablespoons fish sauce *or* soy sauce

1 tablespoon honey *or* syrup

2 tablespoons warm water

1 teaspoon oil

2 scallions, *finely sliced*

EGGPLANT AND TOFU CURRY [Cà Ry Chay]

Serves 4 to 6

When I found eggplant in Carlisle, it was like discovering an old friend.

1 Cut each block of hard tofu into eight pieces. Heat one-half cup oil and sauté tofu until golden.

2 Heat two tablespoons oil in a deep pot and stir-fry garlic, lemongrass and red chile pepper until fragrant. Stir in fried tofu, eggplant, salt, red pepper, sugar, curry powder and tomato paste, and continue to stir-fry for about five minutes.

3 Stir in water, milk, coconut milk, sweet potato, white potato and onion. Simmer for 20 minutes.

TO SERVE: This spicy dish, originally from India, is usually served with French bread in Vietnam. It can also be served with rice.

NOTES:

2 4" x 6" blocks hard tofu and ½ cup oil
or
1 bag (approximately 12 pieces) ready-fried tofu (available in Asian grocery stores)

2 tablespoons oil

2 garlic cloves, *minced*

1 stalk lemongrass, *finely chopped*

1 red chile pepper

2 medium eggplants, *cut into 1-inch cubes*

2 teaspoons salt

½ teaspoon crushed red pepper

2 teaspoons sugar

3 tablespoons curry powder

3 tablespoons tomato paste

1 cup water

1 cup milk

1 cup coconut milk

1 medium sweet potato, *peeled and cut into ½-inch cubes*

2 white potatoes, *peeled and cut into ½-inch cubes*

1 medium onion, *coarsely chopped*

Desserts & Beverages

FIVE-SPICE RICE CAKE [Bánh Xôi Vị]
Serves 8 to 10

This traditional Vietnamese cake is often served for dessert at family gatherings, particularly in rural areas.

1 Soak rice for three hours or overnight in warm water. Drain.

2 In a nonstick saucepan, combine rice, water, coconut milk, five-spice powder, salt and sugar, and bring to a boil. Immediately turn heat to low and using a spatula stir gently for a second or two. Tightly cover saucepan and cook over *very low* heat for about 15 minutes or until done.

3 Line an 8" x 9" pan with foil and sprinkle half the sesame seeds evenly over the foil. Pack rice into cake pan, pressing firmly and sprinkle the top with the remaining sesame seeds. Cool.

TO SERVE: Cut into two-inch squares. Serve with hot tea.

NOTES:

1 cup glutinous rice, *soaked*

½ cup water

½ cup coconut milk

1 teaspoon five-spice powder

¼ teaspoon salt

⅓ cup sugar

¼ cup roasted sesame seeds

BANANA CAKE [Bánh Chuối Nướng]

Yield: 2 loaf cakes

When I last visited Vietnam, my aunt prepared a large loaf of banana cake. I gathered all my friends to talk over tea to enjoy! Using coconut milk means using less butter—it's a different taste, but it's definitely not low-cal.

10 slices white bread

4 eggs

1½ cups sugar

¾ cup flour

2 cups milk

1 cup coconut milk

6 tablespoons butter, *melted*

¼ teaspoon salt

8 bananas, *cut into ⅛-inch slices*

1 Preheat oven to 375 degrees.

2 Remove crusts and cube bread. In the large bowl of an electric mixer, on medium speed, prepare batter by whisking together the eggs and sugar until smooth and light in color. Turn setting to low speed and gradually whisk in bread cubes, flour, milk, coconut milk, melted butter and salt.

3 Butter two loaf pans (approximately 12" x 4½" x 3¼") and line pans with wax paper.

4 Cover bottom of pans with a single layer of banana slices. Top with two ladles of batter. Repeat with remaining ingredients, leaving a half inch of space at top of pans.

5 Bake one hour until golden brown and firm to the touch. Cool on a cake rack.

TO SERVE: Slice and serve with fruit sorbet or jasmine tea.

NOTES:

FLAN CARAMEL [Bánh Caramel Flan]

Serve 6 to 8

This recipe comes from a favorite French restaurant in Vietnam that specializes in making its own ice cream and Flan Caramel. It's a clear example of the French influence in our Vietnamese cooking. Because this recipe uses so many egg yolks, I generally make a batch of Tuiles (page 108), using up the whites.

CARAMEL:

3 tablespoons sugar

3 tablespoons water

CUSTARD:

6 egg yolks

6 eggs

1 ¼ cup sugar

¼ teaspoon salt

2 ½ cups milk

GARNISH:

mango, kiwi, straw-berries, blueberries *or* blackberries

1 Preheat oven to 350 degrees.

2 Caramelize sugar and water over medium heat in a nine-inch round ovenproof pan. Using a wooden spoon, spread caramel evenly over entire surface of pan. Set aside.

3 In a mixing bowl, whisk together egg yolks, eggs, sugar, salt and milk. Pour custard through a fine strainer into the pan.

4 Place flan pan in a large baking dish filled with enough water to reach halfway up the sides of the flan pan. Bake 45 minutes. Custard is ready when it is firm in the center to the touch. Cool custard and refrigerate.

TO SERVE: Unmold flan, by running a thin knife around the inside edge of the pan, and turning out carefully onto a serving plate. Decorate flan with sliced fruit and serve with a few Tuiles (page 108).

NOTES:

TUILES (FRENCH SUGAR COOKIES) [Bánh Tuiles]

Yield: 24 cookies

These cookies are thin, crisp and light. Few folks can eat just one!

6 egg whites

1 cup sugar

1 cup butter, *softened*

⅛ teaspoon salt

1½ cups all-purpose flour

1 Preheat oven to 375 degrees.

2 Beat egg whites with an electric mixer at high speed until foamy, about eight minutes. Gradually beat in sugar.

3 Spoon the softened butter in at slow speed. Add salt and gradually add flour until mixture resembles creamy butter frosting.

4 Grease cookie sheets. To make cookies, use a pastry bag fitted with a large decorating tip, and holding the bag upright, squeeze quarter-sized dollops of cookie dough, two inches apart, onto cookie sheets. Repeat with remaining dough. Bake for about 10 minutes until edges are just beginning to brown. Using a spatula, remove cookies promptly to racks to cool.

TO SERVE: Serve these cookies with your "tea break" or "coffee break"; with Flan Caramel (page 107) or with a scoop of sorbet for a light dessert.

NOTES:

CORN PUDDING WITH COCONUT MILK [Chè Bắp]

Serves 4 to 6

When I was staying with my aunt, "Ma Ba," and her husband, who were inclined to spoil me, they sometimes let me eat a bowl of coconut pudding in the late evening, when I should have been in bed. There are a variety of puddings similar to Corn Pudding. These include Taro Pudding, Black-Eyed Peas in Syrup and Mung Bean Balls. Together we ate these delicious puddings while watching television, savoring every spoonful, and I hope you will too.

1 Combine rice and water in a medium saucepan and bring to a boil. Cook over very gentle heat for about 15 minutes.

2 Stir corn into rice and simmer an additional 15 minutes or until it forms a soft pudding.

3 Meanwhile, place tapioca in a small bowl, cover with warm water and soak for five minutes.

4 Reserve one-half cup coconut milk for sauce. Stir remaining coconut milk and tapioca into pudding and simmer for 10 more minutes. Stir in sugar and salt and continue to stir pudding for two more minutes. Remove from heat and cool.

TO SERVE: Ladle pudding into individual bowls and top each with two tablespoons of Coconut Sauce. Serve warm or cold.

½ cup glutinous rice

2½ cups water

1½ cups corn *or* 3 ears corn, *kernels cut from the cob, with scrapings*

¼ cup tapioca pearls, *soaked*

1 cup coconut milk

1 cup sugar

½ teaspoon salt

COCONUT SAUCE [Nước Dừa]

Yield: 1 Cup

1 In a small saucepan, mix coconut milk, cornstarch and water. Stir sauce over medium heat until it thickens, then add the pinch of salt.

½ cup coconut milk, *reserved from pudding recipes*

1 teaspoon cornstarch

¼ cup water

pinch salt

TARO PUDDING IN COCONUT MILK [Chè Khoai Môn]

Serves 4 to 6

In Saigon, often a vendor would walk along the streets calling out the puddings for sale in the baskets she carried on a pole across her shoulder. Hearing the call, we would summon her in from the street to order the day's puddings. Taro, a large, starchy, root vegetable and a staple in Asia, is becoming available in large supermarkets.

¾ pound taro

½ cup glutinous rice

2 cups water

1 cup coconut milk

½ cup sugar

¼ teaspoon salt

1 Peel taro and chop into one-inch cubes. Cook about 20 minutes. Drain and set aside.

2 In a medium saucepan, combine rice and water. Bring to a boil, turn heat to medium, stir in taro and simmer mixture for about 15 minutes.

3 Reserve one-half cup coconut milk for sauce. Stir the remaining coconut milk, sugar and salt into pudding. Stir pudding about two minutes over low heat. Remove from heat and cool.

4 Prepare Coconut Sauce (opposite).

TO SERVE: Ladle pudding into individual bowls and top each with a few tablespoons of Coconut Sauce (opposite).

NOTES:

BLACK-EYED PEA PUDDING IN COCONUT MILK [Chè Đậu]

Serves 4 to 6

Another vendor favorite.

1 Soak black-eyed peas in plenty of water for three hours or overnight.

2 In a small saucepan, combine black-eyed peas and three cups fresh water. Bring to a boil, turn heat down to medium and cook peas until done—about 25 minutes. Drain and set aside.

3 In a separate saucepan, combine rice and two cups water. Bring to a boil, turn heat to medium. Stir black-eyed peas into rice and cook about 10 minutes. Pudding should look thick and soupy.

4 Reserve one-half cup coconut milk for sauce. Stir remaining coconut milk, sugar and salt into pudding. Stir pudding vigorously about two minutes over low heat. Remove from heat and cool.

5 Prepare Coconut Sauce (page 110).

TO SERVE: Ladle pudding into individual bowls and top with a few tablespoons of Coconut Sauce (page 110).

NOTES:

½ cup dry black-eyed peas

5 cups water

½ cup glutinous rice

1 cup coconut milk

½ cup sugar

¼ teaspoon salt

SWEET GINGERED BLACK-EYED PEAS [Chè Đậu Đen Nấu Gừng]

Serves 4 to 6

Ginger is a favorite home remedy in Vietnam. Whenever we have a spicy dinner, a "ginger-y" dessert or ginger tea is served at the end of the meal.

1 cup dry black-eyed peas

4 cups water

2-inch piece of ginger, *smashed*

1 cup sugar

½ teaspoon salt

1 Soak black-eyed peas in plenty of water for three hours or overnight.

2 In a medium saucepan, combine beans and water. Bring to a boil. Reduce heat to medium low. Stir in smashed ginger and cook 20 minutes.

3 Stir in sugar and salt, and simmer another 10 minutes.

4 Remove the large piece of ginger. Pour peas into individual bowls.

TO SERVE: May be served warm or cooled, and garnished with crystallized ginger. Serve with Tuiles (page 108).

NOTES:

MUNG BEAN RICE BALLS IN BROWN SUGAR SYRUP [Chè Xôi Nước]

Yield: 12 balls

The traditional family favorite!

1 Mix brown sugar, water and ginger and simmer over medium heat about five minutes. Remove from heat and set aside.

2 Soak dry mung beans in a saucepan filled with warm water. Set aside for one hour.

3 In a colander, rinse mung beans and drain thoroughly. Combine water and mung beans in a nonstick saucepan. Bring to a boil, turn heat to medium-low and stir gently for a few seconds. Cover saucepan tightly, turn heat to very low and cook until dry and fluffy. Cool and set aside.

4 Heat one tablespoon oil in a large frying pan and brown onion and scallion. Stir in mung beans, salt and pepper, mashing beans with the back of a large spoon until all ingredients are well mixed. Cool and set aside for 10 minutes. Meanwhile, prepare dough.

5 In a large bowl, mix glutinous rice flour with water. Knead until smooth. Divide dough into 12 even portions.

6 Pour two tablespoons oil into a small bowl and use to lightly oil a baking sheet.

7 Oil your hands and form the mung bean mixture into 12 balls, 1½-inch diameter.

8 Oil the palms of your hands and press each ball of dough into a flat two-inch-wide circle. Center a mung bean ball in the circle and carefully wrap ball in dough, forming a smooth ball. Place ball on oiled baking sheet and repeat with remaining ingredients.

9 Half fill a medium saucepan with water. Add one teaspoon of the

BROWN SUGAR SYRUP:

2 cups brown sugar

2 cups water

2 tablespoons ginger, *thinly sliced*

FILLING:

½ cup dried mung beans

½ cup water

1 tablespoon oil

1 cup onion, *finely chopped*

1 scallion, *finely chopped*

½ teaspoon salt

RICE CAKE DOUGH:

2 cups glutinous rice flour

1 cup warm water

3 tablespoons oil

remaining oil and bring to a boil. Gently add mung bean balls and cook 10 minutes over medium heat. Remove balls with a slotted spoon to a serving bowl.

TO SERVE: Warm the brown sugar syrup, strain, and pour over the mung bean balls. Serve warm.

NOTES:

HOT GINGER TEA [Trà Gừng]
Yield: 2 cups

Following a very old tradition, Vietnamese always serve tea the minute guests enter the house. Various kinds of tea are popular, including black tea, jasmine tea, lotus tea and chrysanthemum tea. My family uses fresh tea leaves instead of dried. Despite the countless types of dried tea available in the United States, I still miss the fresh-leaf tea made in my father's hometown. When anyone was feeling the least bit ill, my mother always made a pot of ginger tea. Tea strongly flavored with ginger is said to be a great remedy for stomach aches and also for head colds. The warmth of the tea, the ginger spice and aroma is very soothing.

1 teaspoon jasmine tea

2 slices ginger

2 cups boiling water

1 Put jasmine tea and ginger in a warmed teapot and pour in the boiling water. Let steep for about five minutes before serving.

NOTES:

ICED LEMON or LIME TEA [Trà Đá Chanh Đường]
Yield: 1 cup

In Vietnamese homes, a full pot of tea, in a specially designed teapot warmer, is kept ready for family and friends throughout the day. It is served with or without sugar, and on very hot days it is poured over ice.

1 cup warm tea

1 tablespoon lemon *or* lime juice

2 teaspoons sugar

6 cubes ice

2 slices lemon *or* lime

pineapple, orange, kiwi, peach, *sliced*

1 Combine tea, juice and sugar, and stir until sugar is diluted. Add ice and fruit slices before serving.

NOTES:

VIETNAMESE ICED BLACK COFFEE [Cà phê Đen Đá]

Yield: 1 glass

In Vietnam children begin drinking coffee at a very young age. My aunt made the most delicious coffee—she and my uncle enjoyed at least five coffee-breaks every day. I was allowed a sip when café au lait was prepared. Coffee drinking soon became a treat.

2 tablespoons Colombian coffee, *finely ground*

1½ cups boiling water

2 tablespoons sugar

ice

1 Using a glass or a clear coffee cup, place a single serving filter on top and add the Colombian coffee. Slowly pour boiling water into the filter and let the coffee drip through. Stir in the sugar until dissolved and just before serving, add lots of ice.

NOTES:

VIETNAMESE CAFE AU LAIT [Cà phê Sữa]

Yield: 1 cup

Preparing coffee in Vietnam is an art in itself. Individual drip filters sit atop clear glass cups and watching the coffee drip slowly drop-by-drop into the glass is part of the enjoyment.

2 tablespoons hot condensed milk
or

2 tablespoons cream and 2 tablespoons sugar

2 tablespoons Colombian coffee, *finely ground*

1½ cups boiling water

1 Pour heated condensed milk, or cream and sugar, into a glass or coffee cup. Place individual drip filter and coffee on top of the cup and slowly pour in boiling water. Stir thoroughly. Ice may be added just before serving.

NOTES:

NOTES:

NOTES: